School Success

The Inside Story

Peter Kline & Laurence D. Martel

LEARNING MATTERS

ARLINGTON VIRGINIA

24.95

How To Use This Book

This book can help you become more successful in all your studies as well as whatever work you may choose to do.

It is based on our years of experience with students, and our observation of the things successful students do that unsuccessful ones usually don't do. If you can learn the behavior of a successful student, you will quickly become one.

Since no two people learn in exactly the same way, we've designed the book to appeal to many different personalities. And we've put in lots of activites, so you can test out what you learn here by putting it to use immediately.

The more you interact with the book, the more you'll get out of it. So we urge you to fill in those blanks, use the space on the page for notes (or doodles), pick some key words, try all the suggested activities, even if they seem unfamiliar or a little difficult at first. These are activities that other people like you have enjoyed and used to make themselves successful.

As you practice what you've learned, you will take charge of your own learning and become the success we know you can be.

Book and Cover Design by Margaret and Mark Esterman

Cover Illustrations by Richard Thompson

Copyright © 1992 by Learning Matters, Inc.
For information contact: **Great Ocean Publishers, Inc.**
1823 North Lincoln Street
Arlington, VA 22207

Library of Congress Cataloging-in-Publication Data
Kline, Peter, 1936-
    School success : the inside story / Peter Kline & Laurence D. Martel.
        p. cm.
    Summary: Presents various strategies for improving the ability to learn, including setting goals, getting organized, and studying with questions.
    ISBN 1-915556-25-1
        1. Study, Method of -- Juvenile literature. 2. Learning -- Juvenile literature. [1. Study, Method of. 2. Learning.] I. Martel, Laurence D., 1943-   . Title.
LB1601.K57   1992
371.3'02812--dc20   92-8120
                                                          CIP
                                                          AC

Printed in the United States of America

Table of Contents

PART ONE: TAKING CHARGE OF YOUR LEARNING

1

Getting The Big Picture

This book is designed to help you learn better, to study better, and to do better in school. Its aim is to make you successful at the things in life that are most important to you. We'll try to make it as enjoyable and as relevant to you personally as we possibly can — because that is the key to successful learning for everyone. In this chapter you'll get an overview of the entire book. So the very first thing you'll know is where you will be when you get to the end.

MAKING THIS BOOK WORK FOR YOU

There are plenty of things about school that could be changed to make it work better for you. We are going to teach you many techniques, tricks, and tips that **you** can use to make some of these changes. As you read, turn on your imagination. See yourself using these new techniques. Perhaps you'll be able to get a glimpse of what school might be like if it were designed to make learning as easy and effective as possible.

See yourself using these new techniques

What's the point of doing this?

Once you begin to imagine an ideal educational experience, you'll be able to create that experience by changing the way you relate to your teachers, fellow students, classroom situations — and yourself.

DOING WHAT THE MOST SUCCESSFUL STUDENTS DO

In the coming chapters, we'll show you many ways to study, learn and think. Once you've discovered the ones that can help you the most, you can put them into practice and breeze ahead.

Keep firmly in mind, that becoming a good student is something ANYONE can achieve. All it takes is knowing what works and what doesn't work for doing homework, studying for a test, taking notes on a lecture, or learning something new.

ANYONE can learn to be a good student

If that sounds like a catalogue of just what you *don't* know — don't worry. These are not mysterious abilities that people either are born with or don't have. They are simply skills that successful students already have learned — and which students who want to be more successful can learn and practice. You are about to learn them, and a lot more that will make you successful.

If you're already a good student, you'll learn a lot more tricks so you can be even better. Then when everything is working properly, and you feel really excited about learning, school can become a lively party, a good movie, and an exciting sports event all rolled into one. But school can't do that all by itself. You have to make it do that.

BUT WHAT'S IT LIKE FOR YOU RIGHT NOW?

At the moment, though, you may not be finding school a wonderful, exciting party. How do you feel?

Here is what school is like for me right now: (Write a phrase or sentence that describes your feelings)

_____

_____

If school feels good to you right now, that's great! But if it doesn't feel so good, just keep reminding yourself that you can learn to be a good student and enjoy yourself in the process.

This book is different from most other books because it focuses on you and asks you to work from your strongest abilities to help you improve your weaker ones. You'll also be learning to take what you already know and apply it to unfamiliar situations. Once you can break down a new situation or idea into a series of well-ordered steps, you will become more successful in your studies.

HOW DO YOU THINK THIS BOOK IS DIFFERENT?

Here is one difference between this book and many other books:

_____

_____

_____

That last question was already answered in the text that preceded it. Perhaps you felt a little insulted when you read the question. You may have noticed it was asking you to copy out some information you had just read in the paragraph before. You may have thought, "If you know the answer already, why are you asking me?"

That's a perfectly natural reaction.

So from now on we're not going to ask you questions like that. We'll ask you questions that require you to think about what sort of answer you'd like to give. There's no right or wrong in the answers we'll be looking for — just your personal opinion. That way you can think through your own reactions to the ideas and situations we'll present you with. It's like a normal conversation between two people, in which each has something to contribute.

There's no right or wrong in the answers we'll be looking for — just your personal opinion.

DO YOU NEED TO BE TREATED LIKE A BABY?

But you might ask, how do I review the facts in the book, to make sure I understand them? We'll solve that problem by asking you to make up the questions. That gets around the whole problem.

This book was designed with especially wide margins. Let's make this book a joint production. These margins are your territory, your contribution to the finished book. You can write your questions and take notes right in the book. We no longer have to test you on the information — you do all the testing yourself. You take the responsibility for what you learn, so no one has to force or pressure you into it.

You did that as a baby learning to speak, *and it worked.*

You can do it now, just as you did then, and learn anything you want to learn. Just let the subject raise questions in your mind, and when you've answered them, you'll have learned the material.

Simple, isn't it?

Well, this book is designed to make learning more simple and pleasant for you.

ANOTHER WAY THIS BOOK IS DIFFERENT

Most books place the Table of Contents right up front, before everything, before the number 1 in Chapter 1. This is a natural place because the table of contents is really a summary of the whole book. The trouble is that most people skip right over it, as if its something they needn't bother to read — and that's a mistake.

This time we're not going to let you make that mistake. We've brought the Table of Contents right into the middle of Chapter 1 and made it the subject of the rest of the chapter. Why? Because the Table of Contents gives you the big picture, that most important overview of the subject.

HOW SCHOOL BREAKS THINGS ALL TO PIECES

One of the most important ways to make learning simpler is to begin by getting an overview of the subject — the Big Picture. If a beautiful vase is smashed to pieces, it's hard to tell what it was supposed to look like before it was smashed. But if you know what it looked like when it was whole, the pieces don't look so strange and it's easy to see how they fit together.

Do you know the story about the elephant in the dark? Once upon a time, four people walking in the dark came upon an elephant. One of them felt the elephant's leg and said it was a tree. A second felt the elephant's ear and said it was a giant leaf. Another felt the elephant's trunk and reported it to be a hollow tube extending down from the sky. The fourth person reached up to the elephant's stomach and found a leathery canopy suspended in space. None of these people knew what an elephant is really like because they could not see how all the parts of the elephant's body go together to make one thing.

Unfortunately, the way things are set up in school, it is often difficult to see how everything is put together. A lot of the time, you probably feel like

You can do your thinking here: write your notes, comments, and questions -- even your drawings and scribbles right in the book.

Key Word

the people who were trying to understand the elephant. You don't have a chance to get an overview and see the big picture, how each part relates to the other parts.

We're going to emphasize the importance of getting an overview of the subject **before** you start working with details. That way you'll always know something about where you're going and what you're trying to accomplish. You probably agree that it's always easier to get somewhere if you know where you're going in the first place. Well, good study really is a matter of knowing where you're going.

STARTING WITH THE TABLE OF CONTENTS

So the first thing we want to teach you is how to get a complete overview of any subject by taking a few minutes to go through the textbook and table of contents.

Let's start with the book you're holding in your hands. We challenge you to a game of picture charades. Without using any words, communicate the main concepts in this book with pictures or symbols.

How to Play the Game

1. Read the titles and subtitles listed in the table of contents.

2. Look for the main idea in each chapter. You may want to circle or underline any words that seem especially important.

3. Then, in the margins of the pages, express the main idea of each chapter with a picture or a symbol. (These are not supposed to be works of art. They can be informal doodles that mean something clear to you. If you know the game of Pictionary, they could be similar to the kind of sketchy picture you would draw in that game to express an idea.)

4. See if a friend or family member can guess what your pictures mean without seeing the words they are based on.

Why are we asking you to draw pictures? Pictures are extremely important in thinking. A lot of our actual thinking is done with images that our brains create. Nearly all great thinkers use pictures to formulate their thinking and to communicate their ideas to others. One good picture can contain a lot of information and also personal meaning and relevance. So if you can sum up this book with your own symbols or pictures, you will have grasped the ideas with your words, your pictures, and your personal feelings too.

SCHOOL SUCCESS: THE INSIDE STORY

TABLE OF CONTENTS

MAPPING BOOKS

Now you're ready to Mind Map — to construct one big picture out of all the little pictures you've created. A Mind Map visually represents the relationships among ideas.

To Mind Map, you write and/or draw the central idea in the middle of the page. Then you arrange the other ideas on branches leading out from the main idea and other branches leading out from these. You look for the connections that make sense to you. Ask yourself which ideas are larger; which secondary and supporting? Then place your lines, words and symbols to represent the decisions you've made. We'll be teaching you much more about Mind Mapping in chapter seven, but here is a Mind Map of this book. Study it, then put your symbols in the circles.

Your Mind Map *shows* how *you* think.

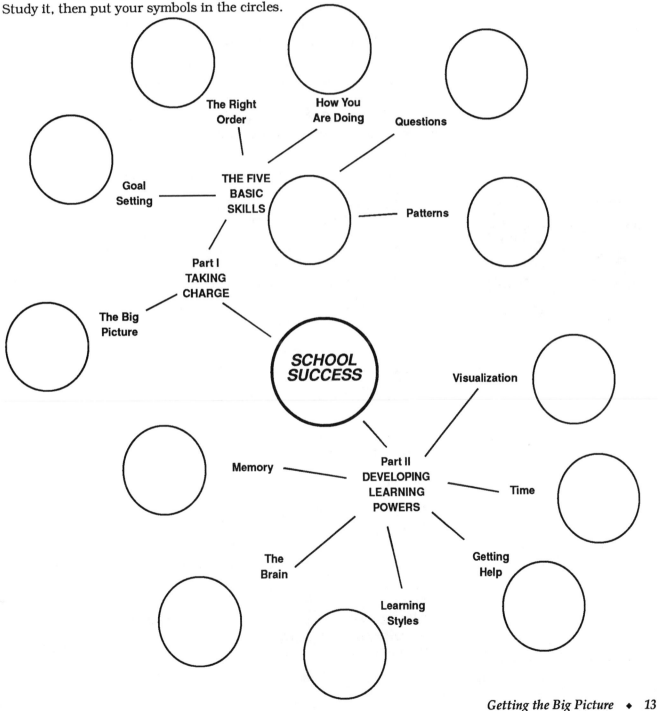

HOW TO MAP ALL OF YOUR TEXTBOOKS

You can do this with all of your school books and get a complete overview of an entire year's work in a very short time.

First go through the table of contents.

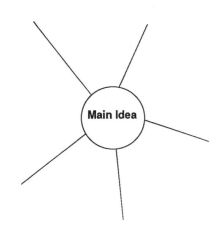

Write the central idea of the book (the book's title is often a good candidate here) in the middle of your paper. Then look for the biggest divisions. Is it broken into **units**? **sections**? or **parts**? Determine the main idea of each unit or part and put it on your map with words and/or pictures.

Then go through the **chapters**. Determine the main idea of each chapter. Think about how they are connected to one another. Are they separate ideas? Are they all secondary ideas to a larger idea? Are some chapters secondary to other chapters in the section? Make these relationships clear in your mind and correspondingly vivid on your Mind Map.

If you're having trouble determining the main ideas in a chapter, you may need to look at more than just the table of contents. Check for special features in your textbooks, like Chapter Summaries or Review Questions. You can look through these and get quick information about what's in the chapter. Then you can finish your Mind Map.

When you're done, you'll have the whole subject beautifully reduced to one single big picture — the whole elephant. You 'll be familiar with all of the pieces and have a good idea of how they all fit together.

PLASTER YOUR TEXTBOOKS ALL OVER YOUR WALLS

You can make a Mind Map poster for your textbook. Hang it up in your room, and soon you'll be thinking about how all the different ideas in the book relate. Then, as you read through the book and study each part, you will feel that you are merely filling in the details of what you already basically understand.

TEXTBOOK TOOLS

Often the authors include other special sections and guides in addition to the table of contents. Chapter summaries, chapter review questions, glossaries, indexes can all help you to read the book more fruitfully.

Chapter Summaries — Many books, including this one, start each chapter with a short summary. When you first get your textbook, read through the concepts at the beginning of each chapter. You'll become familiar with dozens of the major ideas in the course.

Review Questions — Many textbooks include review questions at the end of each chapter. These questions are usually about the most important points in the chapter; the ideas the authors most want you to remember. Go through the list of questions before you read the chapter. Then you'll read with a specific purpose in mind — finding the answers to the most important questions.

Glossaries of Key Terms — These are useful lists that define for the reader the important concepts in the subject. Get to know them before you read. Create on paper or in your mind pictures or symbols that represent these terms.

Indexes — Usually found at the end of a book, indexes help you locate the concepts or names in the book. You can glance through the index and see where and how frequently the key terms are used.

Now we've shown you how to begin your study of a subject by getting the overview of what you're studying. You'll be amazed, once you learn to do this, how much it will help you. In fact, if you didn't follow any of the other advice in this book, this alone could make a tremendous difference.

But this is only the beginning. There is much more you can learn from this book, which we believe will make it easy and enjoyable for you to succeed at school, and at other things that are important to you.

Because if we can make your study time successful for you, you won't want to stop learning, and then nothing in the world can prevent you from becoming the best student you could possibly be.

And that's what we're hoping you'll get from this book.

2

The Five Basic Skills

In this chapter you'll learn about five basic skills that can help you become a super student. You'll get a chance to see what they are, how they relate, and how you can use them most effectively. These skills will be developed more fully in later chapters; but here you'll get an overview of them, so you can understand right from the beginning what you'll need to learn to really excel in school.

THE FIVE BASIC SKILLS

Scientific studies have identified five skills commonly used by highly successful students and rarely used by unsuccessful ones. These are skills that are learned, and can be learned by anyone. And this book will help you learn them. Once you have mastered them, you'll greatly increase your chance to become a highly successful student.

WHAT DO YOU THINK THEY ARE?

Guess what these five skills might be and write your answer here:

_____

_____

_____

_____

_____

Stop! Don't read on till you've filled in the blanks. You'll get the most from this book if you do everything with us as you go. And nobody's watching to see if you make any mistakes.

The reason we asked you to guess the five skills you are going to learn in this book is that guessing what's coming next in a book helps you understand and remember the material you're reading. The five skills we're going to learn about are *goal setting, putting things in the right order, asking questions, finding out how you're doing, and discovering patterns*.

WHY THEY MAKE A DIFFERENCE

There's a good reason why these five skills make such a big difference in school. That reason is YOU!

When you use these five skills, you become an active learner — seeking, directing, developing your own progress. Active learners think for themselves, plan, make decisions, take charge, evaluate, face the facts. By employing the five basic skills, you can actively and successfully accomplish any task or project in school, on the job, or even in your social life. Here's why:

In order to make sense out of your actions you have to decide what it is you're trying to accomplish. That's **goal setting**.

Then you have to divide your task into a series of steps, and decide in what order you will perform these tasks. That's **putting things in the right order**.

Then, in order to understand these tasks, and what you need to know to accomplish them, you'll need to form the habit of **asking questions**.

After that, you can go on doing the task, but you want to **find out how you're doing** as you go, so you don't get too far off track.

Finally, as you get to work, you'll begin **discovering patterns** in the information you're learning and in the skills you are mastering that help you accomplish your goals more effectively.

SET GOALS — COLUMBUS DID TOO

Let's give an example to make this clearer. Suppose you're going to study the voyages that led to the European discovery and exploration of the New World. The first thing you want to do is be clear about the task — set your goal. After all, that's what Columbus had to do. And while he didn't reach the goal he had in mind (finding India) he would never have gotten to America if he hadn't had a goal in the first place.

Like Columbus, you can make new discoveries in life if you set goals for yourself. Otherwise, your life may become boring and repetitive.

Now suppose you've decided to study a chapter in a history book on the voyages of discovery. How is this actually going to get you to your goal? Or, to be more specific, how are you going to study: Do you want to read the chapter and memorize everything in it? Do you want to learn the main concepts involved in the voyages of discovery? Do you want to learn the names of the explorers and the dates of their voyages? You might want to do all of these, or maybe none of them.

But you'll study the material far more effectively if you decide what your goal is in studying it: what you're trying to learn.

Active Learners
Succeed

QUESTIONS TO ASK MYSELF:

What am I trying to learn?

ORGANIZE YOUR TIME

The next thing to do is organize your time so you can get everything done. That means figuring out how many pages you have to study, how long it will take you to study them, what form of study you'll use, and how you'll complete the task. You might decide you have to do three things: read the material, take notes on it and memorize your notes. You then decide whether to finish one before you start the next, or to read one paragraph at a time, take notes on it and then memorize your notes; or to read and take notes all the way through the chapter, and then go back and memorize all the notes at once. That's putting things in the right order.

ASK QUESTIONS ABOUT THE MATERIAL

Your next task is to make up questions as you read your text. We want you to turn your reading upside down. Instead of just taking in information; think about what questions the text is answering. Make these questions as clear and direct in your own mind as you can and write them down. If the questions don't make sense to you, the text won't either. That is why making up questions helps you understand and learn the material. If you ask good questions, you'll discover most of the material you're reading helps to answer them. By asking questions and writing them down, you're organizing the material in your thinking so you can understand it better.

If you're going to ask questions and use the text to answer them, you'll need to allow time for that in your studying. That means revising the order of things in your original study plan. You'll find it's often necessary to revise your plans as you learn more about how to study. That's a good thing, because it shows you're developing new ways to study effectively, and you should keep changing your study plan as you gradually discover the plan that works best for you.

FIND OUT HOW WELL YOU'RE DOING

The next step in building an effective study plan should be to find some way of determining your progress in the task at hand. For example, if you are planning to spend an hour studying the chapter on the voyages of discovery, you'll want to check the clock every so often and make sure you're moving along fast enough. That's one way of checking up on how you're doing. Another is to memorize some of your notes and later go back and review to make certain you remember them well enough. If you check up on yourself in ways like this, you won't get to the end of the task only to discover to your sorrow that you didn't do what you set out to.

NOTICING THE PATTERNS IN THE MATERIAL

When you think about those voyages of discovery, do you notice patterns in them, things common to all the voyages? Did each of them pursue a new challenge that had never been undertaken before? What kind of people sailed on those voyages? From what countries did they come? What were they hoping to accomplish? How did they fund their voyages? These are the kinds of things that may or may not be emphasized in the chapter you're studying. As you notice things like this, you'll come to understand the material better and enjoy it more. That's because the material you have learned will be shaped by your own thinking.

This last of our five skills is perhaps the most interesting. Finding patterns in things around us — in sights we see, in sounds we hear, in thoughts and words — is something we do so naturally that we take it for granted and rarely think about it.

Our natural ability to recognize patterns, and the enjoyment we get from doing it, actually gives us a very powerful tool we can use to study more effectively. As you start to notice patterns in the material you're studying, you understand it better. Instead of a grab bag of information, ideas, and so on, the material begins to take shape — a shape that you give it.

Compare the following two paragraphs:

1. Construct a straight line on a white piece of paper so that the line is three inches long, is parallel to the top of the paper, and has from one of its ends another line going downward two inches in a perpendicular fashion, while from the other end is another similar line also two inches long, going downward in another perpendicular fashion, such that these two lines are parallel to one another and equally distant from each other at all points. Now connect these latter two lines at their bottom ends with a straight line so that this fourth line completes a closed figure which should be describable as a rectangle, making sure that this white piece of paper contains no other unnecessary, stray or overlapping lines.

2. Construct on a white sheet of paper a rectangle three inches by two inches.

You can see that almost all of paragraph number one can be summarized and simplified by using the one word, "rectangle." By recognizing a pattern of four lines as a rectangle you can make generalizations, assumptions, predictions about it. You can find its area, its center, know the size of its angles.

HOW DO WE KNOW YOU CAN DO THIS?

When you were a baby, this is just how you learned. All the information around you was complicated, and as people seldom bothered to simplify it for you, you had to simplify it yourself. You organized the information into patterns that made sense out of the confusion surrounding you.

If that seems like a small accomplishment, think about this: Imagine yourself dropped into a place where you couldn't even speak the language, for example the middle of China (or some other foreign country if you happen to come from China yourself). To make it harder, imagine that you have no idea how the people around you are communicating — with their facial expressions, with the sounds they make, or some combination of methods you don't understand. You don't even know what language is! You don't know *anything* — you're just a baby, in the middle of China.

Well, that is exactly the situation *you* were in when you were a baby. That is how you learned to understand and speak your native language. That achievement alone was much more difficult than anything you will ever have to do in school, yet you did it easily and enthusiastically — because you wanted to, not because someone else told you to.

You also learned how to move your arms, to crawl, and to walk. Soon you learned to run, ride a bicycle, and play sports. You learned to recognize people, use scissors, paint pictures, and do many other things.

LET'S HAVE A PAGE OUT OF YOUR BABY BOOK

Here are three things not mentioned so far that I learned to do when I was a baby:

_____

_____

_____

The ability you had when you were a baby to learn complicated things easily is still inside you. If it does not seem as strong as it was when you were little, that's probably because, like most of us, you got so many "no's" from so many people about your baby activities that you eventually stopped doing them. A lot of the learning skill you had was pushed aside. You began to believe others were right and you were wrong.

You may still feel this way. But now is a good time to trust the power of your own thinking once again and direct the course of your own learning. Set your goals, sequence your actions, check on your progress, ask questions and look for patterns. These are the five basic skills. Use them to become an outstanding student.

But remember, it's one thing to know what they are, and another thing to master them. As you continue working through this book, you will have more chances to practice these five skills. They'll help you get the most from this book and from all your learning experiences.

Try This 👉

Often the best way to learn is to try to teach somebody. We think you will understand a lot more about the five basic skills and learning how to learn if you try the following activity:

Arrange to help a beginning reader to read through a book. Answer any questions your "pupil" may have and observe her or him carefully as the reading proceeds.

Look for the use of the five basic skills. Is there a goal to be reached? Does the reading proceed according to a sequence? What kind of feedback do you need to give? Does the reader need to ask questions? What kinds of patterns does the reader use to decipher the text?

3

Setting Goals

In this chapter you'll have a chance to explore in greater depth the process of setting goals. First, we'll discuss the feeling many people have of not being sure of their goals. We'll see how this uncertainty is caused by conflicts, where they come from, and how resolving them can help us see and reach our goals. Lastly we're going to help and encourage you to think about your goals so you'll know which direction to take. That will give you a tremendous boost in getting more done and doing it better.

Did you know that only a tiny fraction of the people in the world write down their goals in life? That very small group earns the lion's share of the world's money. This doesn't mean you'll get rich just by writing down your goals. But it does suggest that there are some very special things successful people do in order to achieve their success. And when you have acquired these habits, you, too, will be more likely to be successful and get what you want.

_____

_____

_____

Here are three reasons why it might be a good idea to write down my goals:

BUT HOW DO YOU KNOW WHICH GOALS MAKE SENSE?

Setting your goals means taking responsibility for your life. It's true a lot of people don't seem to want to do that. If they can just drift along doing what others tell them, they can avoid thinking for themselves. Following other people's orders may seem to be easier than thinking, but it really isn't. Here's why:

There isn't anyone who can do as good a job of thinking about you as you can yourself. You have more information about your experience and what you've done than anyone else could possibly have. What's ahead of you now is to learn to use this information to help you get what you want.

WHAT MAKES YOU THE WORLD'S GREATEST EXPERT ON YOURSELF?

Here are three reasons why I can think about myself better than anyone else can think about me:

_____

_____

_____

SOMETIMES IT'S HARD TO KNOW WHAT YOU WANT

Have you ever felt that you really don't know what you want? If you are feeling unsure of your goals it could be for one of two reasons: 1) You haven't given it enough thought, or 2) You are in conflict. Let's discuss conflict first.

Imagine, for example, that you are starving and you want to eat, but all the food around you is poisonous. You know if you eat it you'll die. It's hard to decide what to do. You might eat the food anyway and die from the poison, because your hunger is stronger than your fear of death. Whatever you decide, though, is going to leave you in serious conflict, which means it will be difficult to make any decision enthusiastically.

A lot of things in daily life affect us that way. Part of us wants something, and another part doesn't. We may want other people to like us, and at the same time think friendship is too much of a bother. That's a conflict. We may want to do well in school, but at the same time be afraid it will make us unpopular. That's a conflict, too. We may want to earn lots of money, but worry that it will make us feel guilty to have too much.

You can see how there could be thousands of different kinds of conflicts that might make it hard to be clear about what you want.

WHAT CONFLICTS HAVE COME YOUR WAY?

Here are three conflicts I have had to deal with in my life:

_____

_____

_____

There's an important point to remember about conflicting forces. These clashes can prevent something from happening — or they can make it happen more effectively. Forces in conflict with each other are called *antithetical*. That is, they cannot be easily resolved. The process of resolving conflicting forces is called *synthesis*. Synthesizing is relating different, or conflicting, things so they come together as a unified thought, process, or course of action.

When Martin Luther King led the Civil Rights movement, many people wanted to prevent him from being successful. Some used violence against him. King knew the country would not accept such brutal suppression of human rights. Through the media he was able to draw attention to the violence of his opponents.

Many who witnessed the vicious treatment of the Civil Rights protestors on television were outraged, and this made them back King's cause more enthusiastically. So, in some ways, the violent opposition he received actually helped him gain the support of people who might not otherwise have thought his cause important.

SYNTHESIZE! IT'S WORTH A LITTLE BRAIN POWER

Suppose your goal is to get an A in math, but you dislike doing math and spend too little time on your math work.

_____

Here's another subject I feel this way about

This is a conflict that requires a creative solution. Obviously you shouldn't aim for less than an A. So — you'll have to find a way to enjoy doing math.

Here's where the creativity comes in. Maybe you'll need to find the right person to study with, either a teacher or fellow student you can have fun with while working on your math lessons. Maybe using music, or rap or dancing to study math would make it enjoyable for you. Or perhaps combining your math lessons with other things you're doing would help you enjoy it more. It's worth a little brain power to create a solution to conflicts like these.

Visualize . . . your mind will find the solution

_____

_____

_____

Here are some conflicts I should resolve creatively:

The key is to firmly set a goal. Once a goal is clearly stated, the conflicts that stand in the way of achieving it start to dissolve. It's as if by putting extra energy into clarifying the goal, we make the things standing in the way lose some of their energy.

WHEN DID YOU FINALLY DECIDE WHAT YOU WANTED?

_____

_____

Here is a time when I resolved a conflict by making a clear decision about what I wanted:

HOW SMART IS IT TO DO SOMETHING
JUST BECAUSE YOU WERE TOLD NOT TO?

Most of us, adults and children alike, react negatively when we're told not to do something we want to do. When a parent tells a child to stay out of the street, the child may react by wanting to go into it, simply because of having been told no. Possibly you reacted that way when you were a child.

A child who reacts this way enjoys breaking the rule only as long as nothing bad happens. But the rule starts to make more sense if the child gets hit by a car.

Much of the process of growing up consists of accumulating bad experiences that teach us not to do things that aren't good for us. Anyone who can figure out in advance what's good and what isn't can avoid a lot of the pain of having to learn from unpleasant experiences.

Why do we have so much trouble anticipating what might go wrong? Often it's because instead of thinking a decision through for ourselves, we react according to what other people have told us, or what we believe they might think of us. In this way we're giving up our own responsibility and sense of who we are to others, perhaps unwisely.

When we react this way, we may think we're proving our independence. Actually, just the opposite is most likely to be the case: we're showing we can't operate independently and make our own decisions.

IT'S COOL TO THINK ABOUT THE CONSEQUENCES OF YOUR ACTIONS

The best way to prove you're independent is to decide for yourself what makes sense without trying to prove anyone else right or wrong. If you're smart enough to think ahead about the possible consequences of your actions, you can avoid a lot of the pain and misery most people experience in life.

Some of this pain happens as a result of trying to appear "cool" by doing things that only cause trouble. The really cool thing is to think well enough to stay out of trouble, and thus have a more enjoyable and productive life.

Key Word

So declare your independence of knee-jerk, reactive behavior and start thinking for yourself about what will make your life most likely to turn out the way you want it. When you're about to make a decision, think ahead to all the things that can happen as a result of taking that particular action. Then reconsider whether or not the action you've decided on is wise. To guide you in all these decisions you really have to take the time and think about your ultimate goals. Sooner or later you have to decide what you want out of life.

WHAT DO YOU WANT OUT OF LIFE?

We want you to reflect and answer all the questions in the following *Guide to Goal Setting*. The guide asks for your personal feelings and preferences about basic human needs and desires. Certain things about learning — and life — are universal. Everyone wants them. Let's consider the basic desires that all people have in common and then **you** think about your own particular brand of happiness.

TELL US HOW YOU SURVIVE

Survival. If we're in a threatening situation, we will try to escape from it. Imagine yourself surprised by a ferocious tiger that will eat you if you don't run. Do you run? Of course. If a method of escape is not apparent right away, you will invent one in order to survive. Or, to put things on a more general level, you need food and shelter in order to survive. As long as you know you've got them, fine, but you feel very threatened when you don't know where you are going to live, or where your next meal is coming from.

_____

_____

_____

Here are three things I do in order to survive:

_____

_____

Here are three things I'd like to be doing in ten years in order to survive:

YOUR FAVORITE REWARDS

Rewards. It's not satisfying doing something if we get nothing in return for the effort. If we have a job, we want to get paid. If we have a pet, we want it to love and entertain us. If we give a good performance, we want applause. If we don't get rewards for our efforts, we will stop what we are doing and look for something else to do.

_____

_____

Here are my three favorite rewards for doing things well:

_____

_____

Here are the three rewards I'd like to be getting in ten years for doing things well:

_____

WHAT REQUIREMENTS YOU'D LIKE TO AVOID

Control. We all want to be in charge of our own actions. When someone tells us to do something, we want to be able to refuse if the action makes no sense.

Here are three things people sometimes try to make me do that I'd rather not (or three things I wish I could do that I am now prevented from doing):

_____

_____

_____

Here are three things I'd rather not have to be doing ten years from now :

_____

_____

_____

WHAT TURNS YOU ON?

Pleasure. If what we're doing is not interesting or entertaining, we'll find something else to do instead.

Here are three of the things I find most entertaining:

_____

_____

_____

Here are the three things I think I'll find most entertaining ten years from now:

_____

_____

_____

WHAT HAVE YOU DONE THAT YOU CAN BE PROUD OF?

Accomplishments. We all want to feel we've done something important. Would you rather be proud of having written graffiti all over the forest or the subway, or of having written a hit popular song?

Here are three things I am proud of having achieved:

_____

_____

_____

_____

_____

_____

Here are three accomplishments I think I'll be proud of having achieved ten years from now:

NOT SURE HOW YOU'RE DOING?

Feedback. We all want to know how well we're doing. If we can't find out, we feel lost and soon look for something else to do.

_____

_____

_____

Here are three things I've wondered how well I was doing:

WHAT WOULD YOU MOST LIKE TO KNOW?

Explanations. We all want to know how the world works. Some things we simply need to know in order to do what we want to do. When we are confused or mystified by something, we want to discover the rules that explain the mystery. When a magician pulls a rabbit out of a hat, we want to know how the trick was done.

_____

_____

_____

Here are three questions I would like answers to now:

_____

_____

Here are questions or problems I expect I'll be continuing to explore ten years from now:

YOUR FAVORITE TOOLS

We all like having *tools* to help us achieve our goals more easily. Some of us want cars so we can get there faster, or impress people. Some of us want cameras so we can take pictures. But we all want something.

Some tools are things; some are ideas. Here's an example of a tool that is an idea: "If I comb my hair differently, more people will notice me and I will become more popular."

_____

_____

_____

SELF-DISCOVERY

We are all unique and have the ability to contribute to the world in a special way. We all need *self-knowledge* and feel satisfied when we learn about ourselves and discover our talents and abilities. Some of us are insightful about people, some have a talent for working with machines, leadership, artistic talent, great compassion and nurturing ability, skill at communication. The list is endless and comes in as many flavors as there are people. What discoveries have you made about yourself?

_____

_____

_____

_____

If you have sincerely answered these questions you should be closer to knowing what you want out of life — what really will make you happy. Setting your long term goals should be easier now that you're informed with this knowledge about yourself.

Goals should be flexible though. If your goal is too specific, it may prevent you from doing — or even being aware of — other things that could be valuable. For example, if you're hungry, you want to eat. Suppose your goal is going to your favorite restaurant to get a meal. When you arrive there, however, the restaurant is closed. If your goal is too narrow, you could starve to death. This example may seem absurd, but people often suffer, some even for their whole lives, because their goals are so narrow they can't adapt to changing circumstances.

THE DIFFERENCE BETWEEN EXPECTATION AND EXPECTANCY

One way to keep goals flexible is to understand the difference between expectation and expectancy. An expectation is attached to a specific goal, which guarantees disappointment if it's not reached.

Expectancy is directed toward a goal, too, but assumes a lot of interesting and valuable things might happen along the road to reaching the goal. If the original goal is not reached, another, perhaps more rewarding, goal might be substituted.

The person who lives by expectation is rigid and often disappointed. The person who lives by expectancy treats life as an adventure and is seldom disappointed.

YOUR MOST IMPORTANT GOALS

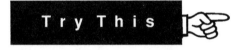

Here are three of my most important goals in life now:

_____

_____

_____

Take this chapter to heart, and you'll be glad you did. You'll be amazed at all the things that will go your way if you are clear about your goals and follow them consistently, determined to reach them and not getting side tracked by friends, activities or issues that are not helpful in achieving them. In the end, what you become will be the result of the goals you set for yourself. If you choose your goals well, you will be the kind of person you can be proud to be.

Try This 👉

Arrange to talk with people who have successfully achieved the goals that you would like to reach. Most people will be very happy to tell you about their path to sucess. You can get a lot of ideas and maybe some encouragement too when you ask these people questions. (Some people may not be able or willing to spend the time with you. But don't be discouraged by this. Look for someone else who can.)

4

Charting The Course To Your Goals

This chapter will talk about how to reach the goals you've set for yourself. What are the steps you need to take to reach your goal? You'll learn how to make a flow chart to help you think through the steps involved. You'll also get some ideas about how to deal with the unexpected and how to prioritize your daily activities to get the most important things done. So let's begin now and think together about what it takes to reach a goal.

Key Word

PUTTING THINGS IN THE RIGHT ORDER

The second of the five basic skills is sequencing — putting things in the right order. Actually, you already do this almost constantly, usually very well. You're doing it now as you read the letters on this page. Your eyes are moving from left to right across the page, taking in the words one by one as you put them together into larger meanings. If you were not doing this, you would not be able to understand the paragraph you are now reading.

Let's look at some other situations in which you naturally arrange things in a good order. You start each day by performing many activities. First you get out of bed. Then you probably use the bathroom. After that, perhaps you take a shower or put on your clothes. What things you do and in what order is something you decide.

In just this way, practically everything you do in life involves putting things in the right order. To decide on the right order, you have to analyze the relationships between the activities. If you could not put things in a good order, you would be in big trouble, because you could not do anything satisfactorily, not even eat a meal.

WHAT HAVE YOU DONE TODAY TO GET ORGANIZED?

Here is one example of putting things in the right order that I actually did today:

_____

_____

_____

ALEX'S ADVENTURES IN ARRIVING AT SCHOOL PREPARED

Alex always came to school before thinking about taking his books with him. When he got to school it was too late to get his books. Then he discovered that if he thought about bringing his books before he left for school, he would have them when he got there. This made life easier for him. He had found the right combination and sequence of events that allowed him to have his books with him when he needed them.

KWANG LEE RAISES HIS TEST GRADES

Kwang Lee always took a test first and studied afterward, in order to learn the information he had missed on the test. As a result, his grades were poor. Then Kwang Lee discovered that if he studied before he took the test, his grades got better. He had found the right combination and sequence of events to help him raise his test scores.

TAMEKA 'S BETTER IDEA

Tameka found that if she prepared for a test by studying a little each night instead of cramming all at once, she did better on the tests. She, too, had found the right combination and sequence of events to help her raise her test scores.

When she learned that she was always scoring higher than Kwang Lee, even after he improved his test scores, she invited him over to her house and showed him how to improve them even more. They also discovered they enjoyed many of the same hobbies, and they soon became good friends. This, too, was an excellent combination and sequence of events for both of them.

DO THESE EXAMPLES SEEM TOO OBVIOUS?

Maybe these stories about Alex, Kwang Lee and Tameka seem too obvious to you. Once we have learned to solve the problems they had to learn to solve, it's hard to imagine that anyone could have such a problem. Yet most of the really serious problems in school often turn out to be as simple as these.

If you're not an A+ student all the time and you want to be, it could be that some very simple thing is standing in your way. Look for your stumbling blocks. Chances are you won't notice them right away, but once you do, they will seem obvious. You won't be able to imagine not knowing them.

WHAT'S THE RIGHT COMBINATION OF EVENTS FOR YOU?

_____

_____

Here is one combination of events, plan or sequence of performing a task that works well for me:

The right combination of events depends on you. No two people study a subject exactly the same way, so your way will be unique — unlike anyone else's.

THE IMPORTANCE OF PRIORITIZING

You can start right now to do things more efficiently by putting your activities into their order of importance for you. We call this *prioritizing*. It is

Key Word

a simple, effective tool that helps you keep on track as you work toward goals, and helps you avoid wasting time on activities that may just distract you.

Make a list of things you plan to do in the next twenty-four hours. Put at least ten of them on the list. They might include: have lunch, go home, study, call my friend, watch TV, read a novel, and so on.

Now, after each item on your list write a number from 1 to 10, indicating how important it is to you. If it's essential, give it a 10, and if it has almost no importance, give it a 1. If you've already decided not to do it, give it a zero.

At this point, some of the things on your list may have the same number after them, but you'll already have a better idea than before of how important each item is to you.

Now copy the list over, but write the items in their order of importance, starting with the most important one. If two or more items have the same number after them, decide which is really more important and list that one first. (You can always go back and rearrange the list later if you change your mind.)

10 Things I Plan To Do Today	The Same 10 Things In Order Of Importance

By making this list of priorities, you will notice that some of your activities deserve more time and commitment than they have been getting, while others deserve less, or perhaps can be eliminated.

Most of us spend too much time doing things that are not important to us, simply because we have fallen into the habit; or because we think someone else wants us to do them. Usually we're not even aware of how much of our time is spent this way.

Prioritizing is a powerful tool to help you plan your activities so you can accomplish what you want to do.

PUTTING THINGS IN THE RIGHT ORDER TO REACH YOUR MOST IMPORTANT GOALS IN LIFE

People who are successful are usually those who have thought through the steps necessary to reach their goal, and then consciously master those steps to the point where they become natural and easy. Their actions might in the beginning have felt awkward or difficult, but over time they have become comfortable habits. Difficult activities become easy when you break them down into a series of manageable steps.

For example, try walking so that every time you take a step with your left foot you pat yourself on the head, and every time you take a step with your right foot you pat yourself on the knee. It would take you at least a few minutes to master this useless task, but it's no harder than your normal way of walking. It's just that it's not what you're used to doing. But after you had practiced each step and formed the new habits you wouldn't have to think about it anymore.

WHAT DO YOU DO WITHOUT THINKING ABOUT IT?

_____

_____

_____

Here are three things I can do without having to think about them:

To master the skills you'll need to succeed in life, you have to teach yourself new habits. Then you can perform at new levels without having to think about it.

Making the effort to learn new skills is like saving money to buy something you want. It takes time and you have to work at it, but in the end you have something valuable. There's a difference, though. If you save money to buy something, you can lose what you have bought. But if you learn a skill and practice it, no one can take it away from you, and you can't lose it.

WHAT HABITS HAVE YOU FORMED?

_____

_____

_____

Here are three good habits I can remember forming:

GO WITH THE FLOW CHART

Next you're going to learn how to flow chart, this is a practical, adaptable skill that will help you to develop a realistic plan for reaching your goals, even very complicated ones. Flow charting will help you to break down the goal into manageable steps, and then to analyze the relationships between the various steps.

What do we mean by the relationships between the steps? We mean the sequence in time (which step first) and the sequence of cause and effect (which step causes which result). Writing it down makes the whole process much clearer. It gives you the overview. Then you can see just what skills you'll need to master and what habits you should be forming to reach your goals.

Here's a flow chart that diagrams in a very simplified way, the process of selecting a college.

Breaking down your goal into manageable steps

Making Flow Charts might look hard, but it's easy -- and they can simplify your life.

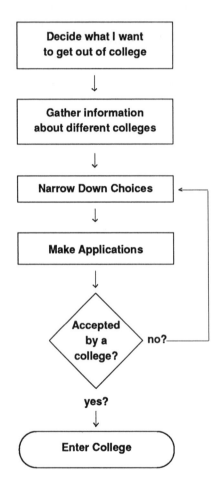

You will notice in this example that three types of boxes are used in flow charting. Boxes with rounded corners are used to indicate the overall goal, in this case, entering college. Rectangular boxes indicate actions to be performed or steps to be reached. Diamond shaped boxes are used to denote points where you may have alternative outcomes. In this example you have to be accepted by a college before you can reach the final step. Arrows connect the different boxes and show how each action leads to the next.

Using these three types of boxes can help you make a better picture of what you have to do, because it helps you decide what the overall goal is, what the various actions are, and what decisions and evaluations have to be made along the way.

The example above was very sketchy and simplified. Really there are many more steps to entering college. You can take each step we mentioned above and make a much more detailed flow chart of the process in each.

Here's a flow chart of step number 3:

Narrowing Down My Choices

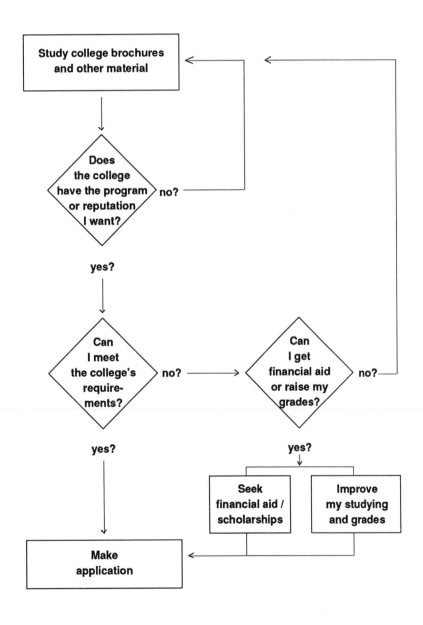

Study this example. Is there anything about it you would change to suit your own needs or goals?

CREATING THE FLOW CHART

When you're creating a flow chart, you put each step in a little box and draw an arrow from that box to the next. If two steps are being pursued at the same time, two arrows should come from the previous step to those that follow it in parallel lines. If, once a step is completed, you can go back to a previous action that had been interrupted, run the arrow back to that action, and move out from it in a new direction, drawing a new set of arrows. In this way, you will show the interrelationships between all the actions involved in reaching your goal. Sometimes the decisions made will change the actions to be taken. Sometimes they are just decisions that have to be made before you can continue.

YOU CAN CHART YOUR OWN SUCCESS RIGHT NOW

Try creating a flow chart for one or all of the goals you wrote in Chapter 3. If your goal is to work in a particular career, for example, these are some of the things you'll want to think about: what training is needed, where to get that training, what is required before you can enter the institutions that give the training, where to get money to pay for the training, what kind of work experience would be useful, what personal attributes should you develop to make yourself more attractive to employers in that field. How you can develop these attributes.

Starting where you are right now and ending with attainment of your goal, try to think of all the steps you must reach along the way. The more complete your list the more accurate and realistic your flow chart will be.

THE STEPS TO MY GOAL

These are the steps I must complete in order to reach my goal. (These will be the rectangular boxes in your flow chart.)

_____

_____

_____

_____

_____

_____

_____

_____

PUTTING THE STEPS IN ORDER

1 _____

2 _____

3 _____

4 _____

5 _____

6 _____

7 _____

8 _____

This is the best sequence in which to perform those steps. (This will be the order and direction of the arrows in your flow chart.)

And so on. You'll probably need to make more numbered steps as you go on.

THINGS I CAN DO AT THE SAME TIME

_____

_____

_____

_____

These steps can be worked on simultaneously. (These steps will be laid out as parallel lines.)

DECISIONS, CHOICES, TESTS

_____

_____

_____

_____

Here is where decisions have to be made, or where requirements must be met, or where I willl be evaluated, or where I will be testing my ideas. These steps will usually pose yes or no questions. (These will be the diamond boxes.)

Some people I can ask for help:

_____

_____

_____

_____

IT'S EASY TO GET HELP TO DO THIS

It will probably be necessary to ask some questions and do some research before you begin. There are people and places that will be glad to help you. Talk to guidance and career counselors, librarians, mentors or people who have successfully reached the goals you are pursuing to find the information that will help you chart your course.

And don't be afraid to ask people who have achieved successes you admire. You'll see that most successful people are happy to answer questions about how they got where they are. And they will know where you're coming from, because they were most likely once just where you are now.

One more thing: Often we are able to reach our goals more quickly because of events we did not expect when we first set out toward the goal.

Even if you design a good flow chart, you don't want to follow it too rigidly. This could prevent you from taking advantage of unexpected opportunities that might develop as you pursue your goal.

EXPRESS YOUR GOAL IN A WORK OF ART

State your goal clearly, make a poster of it, put it up in your room, and let it keep reminding you of the goal you are seeking.

For example, make a poster setting forth your goal in this course, which should be to become a better student who gets more value from school. Decorate the poster with the best pictures you can draw. Put it up on your wall or on the ceiling above your bed to remind you of what you have decided to do. Then your inner mind will go to work to help you reach your goal — by noticing all sorts of things that can assist you along the way, and nudging you to consciously do something about them.

BUT WHAT IF YOU CAN'T MAKE UP YOUR MIND?

Sometimes the problem with goals is that you can't tell at first whether they're good for you or not. For example, you might be trying to decide whether to go to the movies tonight or stay home and make a flow chart that will help you get more out of school. It's not too hard to make a decision about this if you perform the following easy exercise:

Take a piece of paper. Fold it in half. This gives you two columns. At the top of one column write GO TO THE MOVIES. At the top of the other write DO FLOW CHART.

Next write in the appropriate column all the reasons for doing each activity. Once you've written the two lists, it should be obvious to you what will benefit you the most.

After you've used this exercise a couple of times yourself, you can use it to help your friends make decisions they're not sure about.

HOW PERSISTENCE PAYS OFF

If a goal is really important to you, it's worth sticking to it long enough to reach it. Often the most valuable goals take a great deal of persistence.

If things don't always go your way, you may find yourself getting discouraged — but don't give up. The difference between people who enjoy their lives and those who don't often lies most in the ability to keep going when things aren't working out. If you know you're capable of doing so, you'll trust yourself to reach the goals that are important to you.

Key Word

One might say, in fact, that there are two kinds of people in the world — those who have every possible excuse for not doing something, and therefore don't do it, and those who have every possible excuse, but get it done anyway. The point is, if you are going to give up on something, it's easy to find excuses to tell yourself and others why you gave up. But in the end, the excuses won't contribute much to your happiness.

THE JOYS OF EFFECTIVE GOAL SETTING

Perhaps you can now see that finding the right goals and pursuing them effectively is one of the most valuable things you can do for yourself. If you get good at it, you should be able to do just about anything your heart desires.

So why go through life being disappointed that things aren't working out the way you want them to, when by such simple methods you can eventually get them going pretty much in your favor?

Write down the sequence of actions in making a paper airplane (your own design or any standard design). Have someone try to make one using your plans.

5

Finding Out How You Are Doing
So You Know What You Need To Do Next

> In this chapter we're going to explore the concept of feedback. Whenever you're trying to make improvements, it's important to check on your progress, to find out how you are doing. Although it's often possible to get through life doing things less well than we might; it usually makes us happier to do something well. Often it turns out to be easier to do our best than not to. So this chapter will show you some of the many ways you can get information that will help you do better.

FINDING OUT HOW YOU ARE DOING

When you enter a room at night, the first thing you probably do is turn on the light. This lets you see where you're going. Why do you want to see where you're going? Because if you don't, you'll bump into things. This answer might seem obvious, but it is the idea behind all learning experiences. If you can see where you are, you can take a step in the direction you want to go. You can look at what you're doing and decide what to do next.

If you could perfect this one skill alone, you could do anything — anything within human power. If you can get enough information about how well you are doing something, you can then find out what to do next in order to improve your performance. You can keep doing this until you have reached the highest levels of achievement.

WHEN DID YOU FIGURE OUT WHAT TO DO NEXT?

Here is a time when I used information about what I was doing in order to figure out what to do next:

_____

_____

_____

WHAT MIGHT GET IN YOUR WAY?

_____

_____

_____

Here are some reasons I think I might have trouble finding out how I am doing:

THE PROBLEM OF CRITICISM

The trouble is, learning what needs to be done next all too often feels an awful lot like being told we are doing something wrong. And that's not surprising, because sometimes the people who are supposed to be helping us get the two things confused too. What's supposed to be helpful advice comes out sounding like a put-down. Maybe you've gotten this kind of criticism from a teacher, or a parent, or an older student or brother or sister. Maybe you've even given out a little of it yourself.

As we all know, when someone tells us to do something differently, it can seem like we are being told we have failed. Then there's a danger we'll stop trying whatever it is we were learning to do. If that happens, then the person who's trying to show us how to do something better actually keeps us from doing it at all, and that's too bad.

DID CRITICISM EVER HURT YOU?

_____

_____

_____

Here is a time when being told I was doing something incorrectly hurt my feelings and made me not want to go on:

Sometimes criticism may be meant to hurt your feelings. "That's a lousy job!" is not a helpful criticism. The person who says that may just be trying to hurt your feelings.

Actually, a person who says such things might not even want to hurt you in particular. When people are having a rough time, they sometimes try to make themselves feel better by criticizing whoever happens to be around. And people who have been criticized a lot themselves tend to criticize others more.

DID ANYONE EVER TRY TO HURT YOUR FEELINGS?

_____

_____

_____

Here is a time when I think someone may have been trying to hurt me by criticizing me:

Nevertheless, criticsm can be extremely useful in helping you reach your own goals. And if you learn to take criticism well, without being upset by it, there is almost no help that is easier to find and use. Taking criticism well means two things: first, deciding whether or not the criticism is useful, and second, deciding how to apply it if it is. Let's think about this for a few moments:

DECIDING IF IT IS USEFUL

Some criticism is helpful and some is not. Unfortunately, you may get a lot of criticism from people who don't understand what you're trying to do. You may also get criticism that is too general to be helpful. For example, saying "you're not doing that well enough" is too general because it does not tell you specifically how you could improve.

WHEN WAS CRITICISM OF NO USE TO YOU?

Here are two examples of criticisms I've received in the past that were too general to be helpful:

_____

_____

For example, grades by themselves are often not helpful. If you get a D — with no comments — on a paper, it means that the teacher doesn't think you did very well but hasn't told you why. The D by itself is not helpful. You need additional information. The D is mainly an indication that you need to get more information about how to improve your work.

HOW DOES BEING GRADED REALLY MAKE YOU FEEL?

Here is how I react when I'm graded on something I've done:

_____

_____

WHEN CRITICISM IS IRRELEVANT

When people criticize you without understanding what you're trying to do, even when their criticism is specific, it won't help much either. Suppose someone criticizes a boat you're building because it doesn't have any wheels. The person might give you detailed information about what kind of wheels are needed, how big they should be, and so on. But the criticism doesn't help you improve the boat one bit.

This example might sound far-fetched, but it's just like a lot of criticism people actually do give each other. Unfortunately, because people often don't understand each other's purposes or goals, there is a lot of criticism around that isn't helping anyone. Teachers, being human like the rest of us, sometimes give irrelevant or erroneous criticism too.

ARE YOU EVER MISUNDERSTOOD?

Here is a time when someone criticized me in a way that showed a misunderstanding of what I was trying to accomplish:

_____

_____

APPLYING IT IF IT'S USEFUL

If the criticism seems useful, however, it makes sense to learn as much as you can from it.

Let's suppose you feel bad about not having as many friends as you'd like and someone says to you, "People don't like you because you're mean to them." If this criticism is true, it's also useful. If you're mean to others, you won't have many friends. You might not even be aware you're being mean to others, and therefore you might not know why you don't have as many friends as you'd like.

So even if it hurt your feelings to hear about your meanness, it would help you feel better in the long run, because you would know that you need to change your behavior to get more friends.

HAVE YOU EVER USED THE GIFT OF GOOD CRITICISM?

_____

_____

Here is a time when I applied some criticism I received and it helped me do better:

COULD CRITICISM ACTUALLY HELP YOU?

_____

_____

Here is a criticism that really might help me understand what I need to improve:

CHECKLIST FOR FINDING OUT HOW YOU ARE DOING

1. Ask specific questions. The question, "How am I doing?" is not very helpful, because it does not direct the person to give you the exact information you need.

2. Ask about the work that's going well. You want to be sure to keep doing those things in your work that are already successful, and not leave them out, or change them to something else. So ask, "What are the five best things about my work right now?" Write down the answers and pay close attention to them. These are the things you don't want to change. Also, knowing there are five things you are doing well will help you feel good about changing some of the things that aren't working so well.

3. Next ask, "What is the one thing I most need to add out of all that's missing?" The reason to concentrate on one thing at a time here is to keep the focus clear. Make sure you thoroughly understand what one thing needs to be added in order to improve your work, and take the time to understand it completely before you go on.

To make sure you're clear about what you need to change, it might be good to have the person explain it in several different ways. Then explain it back in your own words and see if the other person agrees.

4. Next, try to find out about another quality that's missing from your work and needs to be added. Again, take the time to understand fully what that is. When you have done so, ask for another quality in your work that can be improved.

5. Now that you've got a picture of what's already good and what needs to be added, ask if there's anything that needs to be taken out. This will provide you with information on what you're doing that is not helpful in your work.

6. Once you've gotten all the information you think you can absorb right away, say, "Thank you very much for your help. I think I have about all the information I can handle right now."

7. If there's more you need to learn about how to improve, you can always learn that later. Trying to learn too much at one time will not be helpful. If you have already been given more information than you can handle, then simply put part of it aside and decide what you are going to do first to make some improvements in your work.

PROBLEM SOLVING — FIGURING OUT WHAT TO DO NEXT

Here's where finding out what needs to be done next comes in. You've got to know *what* you need to do, and figure out *how* to do it. In a previous example, what you needed to do in order to have more friends was to start being nice to people. But, you might wonder, what does being nice to people mean?

That's what you have to figure out in order to know what needs to be done next. You have to learn what makes people happy. Then you can change your behavior to accomplish your goal. By finding out how to be nice to people, you figure out your next step.

HOW TO IMPROVE THROUGH TRIAL AND ERROR

The most basic way to decide what to do next is through trial and error. Let's think about how that might be applied in your situation.

Suppose you're failing a course. Maybe you go to class, do all your homework and study hard. But somehow when it comes time to take the test, you fail. The feedback you're getting, failing grades, shows that you have to try something else.

Let's assume there's something you haven't tried. Sit down with yourself or someone else and try to decide what is causing the problem. You can do this quite easily if you'll just take a few moments to ask yourself questions. See if you notice any patterns in your behavior that might be causing the trouble. This will help you form some ideas about possible causes of the problem.

When you have an idea, an hypothesis, about the cause or causes, you can say to yourself, "If I do such and such, I might correct this problem." Then list the actions you need to take, and put them into the right sequence for correcting the problem.

Now you have a plan of action. You can actually do something. So try it for a while. Then get new feedback.

Here's a comic strip of someone coming up with the solution to a nagging school problem:

How about trying to put in the words for a comic strip about finding a solution to a problem you may be having?

THE ALTERNATIVE TO GIVING UP

What if the new feedback reveals that your plan is not working?. At this point, many of us would give up. We would say, "I tried to solve the problem, but my solution did not work, so things are hopeless."

But there is an alternative. Study the problem again and decide what else may be wrong. Then form another hypothesis and test it out. Every time you form an hypothesis and test it out, make sure you get feedback on your work. This feedback helps you determine which of your efforts are successful and which are not.

If you form enough hypotheses and test them out, you will eventually find a solution, or a combination of solutions, that works.

If you are to be successful at this, the most valuable thing to do is keep forming hypotheses and testing them until you get the results you want. This might seem like a tall order. It might take a long time to go through the whole process, but there will be hidden benefits which you will discover only after you've tested a number of ideas.

HOW YOU CAN BECOME A PROBLEM SOLVER

After you've been through this process a few times, you'll have learned some techniques of problem solving that can help you in almost any situation. If you become skillful at improving your schoolwork, what you learn about problem solving will help you in other facets of your life, as well.

Actually, there is a great deal you can do to improve the responses you get from other people, but you need to pay close attention to what these are. If you pay attention to what your senses and intelligences are telling you, you will know more about how well you are doing, and will be able to use this information to improve your performance in anything.

Here is a part of my life that is not going well:

_____

_____

Here are some possible reasons that I'm having this problem:

_____

_____

Here are some actions I can take to make the problem better:

_____

_____

WHY WE HAVE TROUBLE USING THE FEEDBACK WE GET

We all tend to have two emotional responses that prevent us from either seeking out or paying attention to useful feedback: denial and despair. Let's consider each of them.

Of the two, denial is more serious. In denying our problems, we only ensure that they will continue. We deny things when we are so afraid to face them that our only recourse is to tell ourselves they do not exist.

Pretending things are good when they are not is something you probably do from time to time, too. The sad result is you usually won't try to improve the situation.

THE PROBLEM WITH DENIAL IN SCHOOL

Denial is also very common in school situations. If you are not doing well in your schoolwork, you can do one of three things. You can feel bad that you are not doing well, you can deny that it matters to you, or you can pretend that what you are doing is actually good enough.

If you feel bad that you are not doing well, you can then find out what you need to do to improve. If you pretend that your work is good, though, you will ignore any useful feedback you may get, and will continue to do poorly.

HOW DESPAIR PREPARES THE WAY FOR FURTHER DESPAIR

The second cause of ignoring feedback is despair. Despair is a feeling of helplessness, that nothing you can possibly do will be good enough or can correct the situation.

School situations can occasionally lead to despair. You might come to the conclusion that some part of your schoolwork is so difficult that, no matter what you do, you cannot improve. But even in school — especially in school — there are ways to get help and learn what you need.

THE MISTAKEN IDEA THAT YOU'RE NOT SMART ENOUGH

Most people go through life performing at more or less the same level. This is so common that a mistaken impression has arisen (even among some psychologists) that intelligence is more or less fixed at birth, and one cannot become significantly more intelligent as one grows up.

It is now known, however, that intelligence may vary a great deal throughout a person's life. For example, there is a case on record of an eighteen year old who had an I.Q. of 50, barely enough for a person to function outside of an institution for the mentally retarded. After several years of a specially designed educational program, this young man raised his intelligence sufficiently to become a college professor.

> Your intelligence can grow.

You may know many people who do better work in school than you do. Probably most of them have been doing about the same level work throughout their lives, and will continue to do so in the future.

It is possible, though, for any particular person to change his or her way of thinking so that intelligence actually increases over time. This occurs as we change the way we process information.

GETTING SMARTER BY LEARNING BETTER

So, just for the sake of argument, let's say you are a student who has always done poorly in school. Perhaps you are several grade levels behind, and feel you will never learn to read well and will always do poorly in most subjects.

But then, let's say you learn some techniques that change the way you think and study. As a result, you can improve each day. If you keep improving, not just in knowledge, but also in the ability to learn, you will eventually overtake many of your classmates who have always been better students than you. Soon enough you may out-perform them. Furthermore, you can keep getting better and better for as long as you wish, because you will be improving not just your learning, but also your rate of learning.

It's as if another person were walking along a flat plain while you climbed a hill. You would keep climbing higher and higher while the other would remain at the same level. Just so, your learning can get better and better while another's remains at the same level.

So it doesn't matter where you start out when you're learning something; it matters how effectively you learn. If you're not very good at something but figure out how to do better at it, you'll learn the process of getting better at things. You can then apply this process to any situation. Thus, you could move from a D or an F in a subject to a B or an A. And once you've accomplished that, you can keep moving and do better than A work. Anyone can accomplish this, given the right study methods.

Try This 👉

Giving meaningful feedback can be as valuable an experience as getting it. Here's a chance to practice giving us some much needed feedback. We — the authors of this book — would like to know how we are doing so we can improve it.

On the facing page is a questionnnaire about the book. You might want to wait till you've finished the whole book before you answer it. The page is designed so that if you remove it from the book and fold it and tape or staple it as instructed on the other side, you can simply put a stamp on it and drop it in the mail to us. (You can also copy this page, or write your feedback on another piece of paper and send it to the same address if you prefer.)

If you'd like to add anything, or simply to send us your opinions without answering these specific questions, that would be fine too.

We will try to respond to all of your feedback. And we will certainly acknowledge any suggestions of yours that we use in future editions of the

Feedback to the Authors of *School Success*

What did you like best about this book? _____

_____

What did you like least? _____

_____

What was hard to understand? _____

_____

What was too easy for you? _____

_____

What do you think should be changed? _____

_____

What do you wish were in the book that isn't there now? _____

_____

What would you like us to remove from the book? _____

_____

How could the book be made more helpful to you? _____

_____

Tell us a success story based on something you learned in the book. _____

_____

Tell us something you read about in the book and tried, but found it didn't work. _____

_____

Are there enough things for you to do? _____

_____

What activity did you like best? _____

_____

Were there any things to do that you didn't like? _____

_____

How do you think this book might help others in ways that you yourself don't need any help? ____

_____

Would you tell your friends to read this book? _____

_____

Can you think of a book designed to help you study that you like better than this one? _____

_____

Are there things in other books that you think we should have included in this one? _____

_____

FOLD HERE

From: _____

Home Address: _____

_____

City / State / Zip _____

PLACE
POSTAGE
STAMP
HERE

Peter Kline & Laurence Martel

$^c/_o$ LEARNING MATTERS, INC.

1823 North Lincoln Street

Arlington, VA 22207-3746

FOLD HERE, AND FOLD THIS PANEL UNDER TOP PANEL

Any other comments? _____

_____

_____

_____

_____

6

Becoming An Active Learner

This chapter is about questions and how to ask them. Effective question asking is one of the best tools we have to increase our knowledge and skill. If you just answer other people's questions, chances are you're a passive student. But if you ask questions yourself, you'll be well on the way to being an active student who has control over the learning process. So get set for a wonderful time exploring the possibilities of question asking.

Good students are active learners. They don't just sit around waiting for learning to happen — they make it happen. They know they can learn, and they do learn — in any class, no matter how badly taught, and in any situation.

WE ALL STARTED OUT ON THE RIGHT TRACK

Everyone starts life as an active learner. That's how all of us learned to speak, and that's how you, in particular, learned to speak. After months of listening to the words that other people used, you started putting words together yourself. You invented your native language in your own way. That's why no one else uses words exactly as you do — you have a unique voice.

You learned to crawl, to stand up, to walk.

You learned these and many other things because you wanted to learn them. This desire made you ask the people around you for help.

You did all this because active learning is an instinct you were born with.

ASKING GOOD QUESTIONS IS
PART OF PURSUING YOUR GOALS EFFECTIVELY

You can't get anywhere without asking questions. As you pursue your goals and try to understand more about the world you are creating for yourself, you'll need new information. The more you form the habit of asking questions and learning from everyone you meet, the more powerfully your thinking will develop.

Don't be afraid to ask questions because you think people will think you are not very smart. Only the smartest people know how to ask really good questions, and the people who ask them and get good answers are constantly getting smarter. So can you.

Besides, it's born into you to be a question asker. Unfortunately, however, some of your youthful excitement about discovering new things may have been crushed by other people not wanting to answer your questions. As a baby, you probably liked to plunge merrily ahead, taking on each new challenge with excitement. Almost as soon as you could talk, you started asking questions. Maybe a lot of them were answered well, but you probably heard plenty of answers like: "That's a stupid question," or "Don't bother me, I'm busy," or "Why do you ask questions like that?"

WHAT WERE THE GREAT QUESTIONS IN YOUR YOUNG LIFE?

Here are three questions I asked when I was little that I never got good answers to:

_____

_____

_____

Despite what people around you might have said, all of your questions were intelligent. They were what you needed to know at the time, and you naturally wanted truthful, understandable answers. As time went on, you probably became discouraged about asking questions, maybe even afraid.

RECLAIM YOUR BIRTHRIGHT

So remember — **learning happens when you make it happen**.

Let's start making learning happen more actively for you right now — in school. Let's begin by exploring in more detail the art of asking questions — the probing, interesting questions you often asked when you were a child, before people shut you up by calling you a pest, or made you feel your questions were stupid, your ideas no good, or your desires foolish. Of course, maybe none of that happened to you, and if it didn't you're lucky.

HOW TO STUDY WITH QUESTIONS

You've probably noticed how we've been using questions in this book. We started out by asking you lots of them. Gradually, we're trying to get **you** to ask more questions for yourself.

Posing thoughtful questions about a problem is always an important first step toward a solution. If you can mentally step back from your situation, look at it objectively, and ask the right questions, you can figure out how to solve almost any problem you may ever have to face. That's what it means to be an active learner.

Here are some things I hope to gain by improving my ability to ask questions in all situations:

_____

_____

INTRODUCING THE MAGIC QUESTION MACHINE

Here's why asking questions can really help you. Each good question you ask focuses your attention on some new idea you have not yet completely understood. The question prepares you to understand and remember new information.

In effect, you are a magic machine for asking questions — because your questions are so valuable to your thinking, they have an almost magical effect on your ability to improve your understanding and schoolwork.

THIS BOOK NEEDS TO BE IMPROVED — BY YOU

As you've probably noticed already, and as you will see as you browse through this book, we encourage you to react to and interact with it as much as possible. We'd like you to pepper this book with your questions — so you'll then go on and do the same to other books.

For that reason we've tried to leave places on the pages for you to personalize and elaborate on ideas you find in the book, and margins where you can make notes or doodles or whatever else you feel inspired to. This is meant to be a workbook — or better still, a playbook — which you'll get more out of, the more you put in. (We *don't*, of course, recommend you do this in books that don't belong to you.)

In this chapter we're going to emphasize that you use these margins for jotting down questions which the text raises in your mind. You can do this anywhere in the book, but for the moment we suggest you do it here.

WHY IT'S BETTER TO BE AN ACTIVE READER

As you read along in this book, or any other, you should be aware of what questions the authors are trying to answer. When you ask yourself *"what questions are being answered here"*, you make yourself an active, instead of a passive reader. Because by reading this way, you are asking not only *"what* are the authors saying?" but *"why are they saying this?"* and *"how does it fit in with the rest of what they are saying?"*

Make yourself an active reader by being aware of what questions the authors are trying to answer.

There may be places where you can't understand either the meaning or the purpose of what you are reading. Those could be extremely valuable places for you, because they allow you to focus on what you don't understand or need to learn. You don't want to pass over those spots — you need to find them and pursue them. It may be that you are missing something vital that a teacher, or another reader, could help you understand.

Or it's also possible that the authors themselves have a problem. Perhaps they are falling down on the job, or skipping some important step, or failing to be clear about what they are trying to say, or about information you need. In that case you may want to pursue the question with another reader, or a teacher — or the authors themselves.

IS ACTIVE READING WORTH THE EFFORT?

Does this seem like more than you want to know about your reading, like an extra chore added on top of all your other work? It's not. It's actually a way of making your reading and your studying more efficient, of making every author your personal teacher.

Because when you read actively you are not only understanding what you read more fully, you are making that information your own, fitting it in to what you know and what you need to know. Think of opening a book as going to a great restaurant. Instead of smelling the food as it goes by on a tray, you're really tasting, chewing and digesting it.

So, is it worth the effort? Do you want to learn the very things you need to know to do well in any course in a way that will make that knowledge a part of you and easy to remember?

TRY THIS

If it's not something you're already doing, try this: In the margin next to some paragraphs of your choice in this chapter, write at least two questions answered by that paragraph. You might also want to write questions not answered by the paragraph that you may wish to investigate on your own.

You will see that sometimes questions that are not answered by the paragraph are answered later in the text. Writing questions about one paragraph that are answered by another helps you think about what is coming in the text and thus understand better how the material in the course is being developed.

SOME SAMPLES TO GET YOU STARTED

To get you started, here are sample questions for the section above that you have just read, following the heading, **TRY THIS**. For practice, go back and write them in the margin. Feel free to rephrase or change the questions. For each paragraph, the first two questions below are answered by the paragraph, and the third is not.

The following questions would do for the first paragraph:

1) *How should I practice asking questions in this book?*

2) *Do all the questions I ask have to be answered in the paragraph?*

3) *Suppose nobody knows the answer to my question?*

Now for the second paragraph:

1) *Will my unanswered questions be answered later in the book?*

2) *What is the value of asking questions not answered in the paragraph?*

3) *What do I do if asking questions only confuses me?*

As you read through this chapter and the rest of this book, try doing this with other paragraphs or sections. Try it even if it seems mechanical or tedious at first. You'll soon see that being an active reader doesn't have to be dull. You can turn it into something interesting and useful to yourself, leading to questions, ideas, directions that mean something to you (and probably to other people as well). That is the power of questions.

You can do this with every paragraph, but in case you forget, we'll remind you every once in a while in this chapter.

DO THE SAME WITH LECTURE NOTES AS YOU DO WITH BOOKS

When you attend a lecture, try to write down all the points the lecturer is making. After the lecture, go back and write questions in the margins of your notes. This will help you organize the lecture in your mind so you can remember it better.

When you come to reviewing the material, or studying for a test, read over the questions and see if you can answer them without reading the answers in your notes or text. When you compare your answers with those that are written down, you will immediately know how well you did.

WHAT GOOD NOTES WILL DO FOR YOU

This brings us to the question of taking notes. Good notes have two important purposes. They are first of all a record of the class lectures. Additionally, good notes are a personal set of thoughts about your studies that you put down on paper.

Notes are not so much for the purpose of memorizing, as for the purpose of processing the information in your mind. If you learn to do this well enough, you won't need much review. By putting each new idea into your own words, you are forcing yourself to think about it and understand it better.

If you want an even better way to help you remember the ideas, go through your notes soon after you've taken them, and draw pictures to help you remember them. These pictures will work best if they're very simple doodles that capture some of the idea you've written. For example, if you encounter the word "love", you can draw a heart. See if you can find simple visual symbols of that type for each of your ideas. A little practice will make you much better at this, and soon you'll be able to remember large numbers of ideas by remembering the pictures that go with them.

In the process of note taking, you'll want to develop some additional skills that will help you get the most out of the experience. Here are some observations that may be helpful:

THE THREE BASIC SKILLS OF NOTE-TAKING

Note-Taking: You are *not* going to attempt to organize your notes while you take them. You're going to write down every important thing that happens or is said in the class. This will give you a complete narrative of the class.

This method of note-taking eliminates the difficulty of trying to do two things at once: taking in information and organizing it at the same time. If you will concentrate during a lecture or discussion on just noticing what is said, you can then think about it and organize it later.

You'll learn, as you improve your skill, that there are natural pauses in the flow of discussion during which you can ask questions or participate without having to be writing at the same time.

When we say write down every important thing, we don't mean everything word for word. That is usually not practical or possible. So find ways that you can make a record that makes sense to you. Use abbreviations to save time. Learn the standard ones, and make up additional ones of your own. Pretty soon you'll have your own personal shorthand that gets things down on paper quickly.

As you're taking notes, record all the information in the lecture or discussion. If you don't hear something, put a question mark and fill it in later, maybe after asking a question about what was said at that point.

Question-Raising: After you've taken the notes, go over them and ask questions which the notes themselves answer. This will get you thinking about the meaning of what you've reported on. Nothing, after all, is of any use to you until you know what it means. By asking questions you'll be preparing your thoughts for the third step, which is:

Synthesizing: Here you rearrange the notes into a set of patterns that are meaningful to you. Create a mind map based on your questions or construct a diagram or an outline showing the interconnections between related ideas. You learn the most by noticing patterns and relationships in the material you're studying. (You'll be learning Mind Mapping and many other pattern recognition skills in Chapter 7.)

This method, which is similar to the famous Cornell note-taking method, allows you to move quickly and easily from one step to another without having to struggle or think too hard. It's best done by leaving room in your notes for questions that occur to you at the time or later.

For example, on a normal $8^1/_2$ inch piece of notebook paper leave a three inch margin on one side, as in the example below. This way you can write down everything that happens in your class in the main section of the page, and still have room for your questions in the margin. While you take notes, then, you won't have to think or analyze — just write. Being a good reporter, you see, is the first building block to learning.

Sample division of lecture note page

Write in this area during the lecture

Use this area when you write questions or organize your notes

THREE TYPES OF QUESTIONS

Now let's think about three different kinds of questions you can ask.

1) Empirical Questions. These questions ask for information contained in the material you're studying. An example of an empirical question based on this paragraph is, "How many words are in this paragraph?" They are questions to which the answers are factual, and are contained in the world around us. They seek proof or evidence as their answer.

2) Value Questions. These questions reflect values or point of view. Often when you answer a value question you're giving your opinion. Empirical questions do not ask for your opinion, but value questions do. Empirical question: "Who's the author of this passage?" Value question: "How did you enjoy this passage?" Value questions are useful in setting standards.

3) Analytical Questions. These questions ask for a definition of what we mean by the words used in the question. Often they need to be asked before the other two types of questions can be answered. For example, consider the question, "If a tree falls in a forest where there is no ear to hear, does it make any noise?" In attempting to answer this question you have to ask another one first: "What is meant by the word *noise*?" When this analytical question has been answered, the empirical question is then easy to answer. If the word *noise* means vibrations in the air caused by some event, then the answer is yes. But if *noise* means "the effect of air vibrations on an ear drum and the interpretation of these by a brain," then the event makes no noise. The purpose of analytical questions is to determine the meaning of something.

Everything we study requires us to use all three of these types of questions.

HOW ELROY BECAME A WHIZ AT TAKING LECTURE NOTES

Elroy Johnson was in the sad position of failing all his courses in school. Whenever the teachers gave lectures, his mind wandered. He thought about his friends and his tape collection and what his girlfriend would be wearing Saturday night. But he did not think about the teacher's remarks on the impact of hydrochloric acid on the four food groups in the digestive system. Somehow the digestive system never held his attention, except when he was hungry.

Elroy's girlfriend, Mabel, was a straight-A student who was embarrassed to be seen going out with some guy who was flunking all his courses. So, because she loved Elroy, she decided to help him become a straight-A student too.

MABEL'S TRICKS FOR TAKING NOTES

"It's really very simple, Elroy," said Mabel. "You only need to learn a few tricks about taking notes during lectures. First of all, you want to get down on paper everything the teacher says."

"He talks too fast," said Elroy.

"It only seems that way because you're not writing fast enough. Here are some ways you can get everything down. If you get behind, leave some space in your notes so you can go back later and add the missing information. You can ask someone else what was said in that place, or it might even come back to you as you're thinking about it.

"Next, figure out abbreviations for the words you write most frequently. Reduce common words to single letters with special signs. For example, *with* could be written as a *w* with a line under it or a slash after it, like this: *w*, or *w/*. Be sure to learn abbreviations for all the key words in the course you're taking. Never write *biology* if you could write *bio*. Create your own glossary of abbreviations in a notebook.

"Make sure there's lots of margin space in your notes. Also, take notes on only one side of the page. Then go back and write in questions about the notes. This will help you organize the lecture in your mind and remember it better. Writing questions is also a great way to review your lecture notes. When you're studying for a test, cover the notes and just try to answer the questions. You can always read your notes for any answers you don't remember."

HOW ELROY'S UNDERSTANDING IMPROVED

Elroy tried all Mabel's suggestions, and, sure enough, he began to follow what his teachers were saying. He did so well with his lecture notes that he was soon understanding the material much better. He even started looking forward to class because, now that he understood the material, he was getting interested in his subjects.

As time went by, he found he could pay attention to lectures even when he wasn't taking notes, because he had trained himself to listen in a more organized way.

HOW ELROY LEARNED TO EVALUATE LECTURES

Still, in order to be a really top student, Elroy needed to evaluate the information in the lectures. He had to decide what was important and what was not. He did this by discussing the ideas in the lectures with other people and by thinking about the overall effect of the lectures. At first, he would get sidetracked on unimportant points, but with practice he got better at seeing how all the details of a lecture fit together.

Elroy sometimes found that teachers did not organize their lectures well and got sidetracked themselves, introducing unimportant or irrelevant issues and not covering the material they said they would cover. Elroy learned to distinguish between well-organized lectures that got to the point and those that rambled and didn't lead anywhere. Nevertheless, he was still able to learn from rambling lectures. That was because his notes were thorough, and his questions in the margins helped him focus on what was of value in a lecture, even if he sometimes had to dig for it.

Thanks to his new note-taking technique, Elroy was soon getting A's in most of his courses. Elroy discovered that many of his own questions were the very same ones the teacher asked on the tests. Everything was easier. And now Mabel was very proud to go out with him — particularly because she had helped him so much.

LEARNING TO THINK LIKE A NEWSPAPER REPORTER OR A DETECTIVE

We encourage you to develop the attitude of a newspaper reporter as an aid to understanding what is happening around you. Try to get to the bottom of the story.

When you become a good reporter and questioner, you can more easily understand and interpret what is going on around you. As a result, you'll be better able to contribute something valuable to any situation you participate in.

In a sense, you're learning to be like Sherlock Holmes. Holmes studied the clues to a mystery in order to discover what was happening. Often his unique individual point of view allowed him to solve mysteries that the police from Scotland Yard could not solve.

By learning to ask good questions, you'll start to see clues you would otherwise miss. Think of your teachers as if they were giving testimony in a murder trial. You are taking down the testimony and are going to examine it to see whether it is true or not. You will compare it with what you have previously learned and what you can read about. Focus on the larger patterns: what ties everything together — where is the discussion leading — what does the teacher seem to be driving at? What's the point?

You will think about it. You will form a theory or idea about what is really true. You will test out that idea and come to your own thoughtful conclusions, always keeping an open mind to new, additional information you might need to consider.

QUESTIONING THE STATUS QUO

As you become good at questioning and start trusting your ability to "own" ideas and start to develop your own purposes in learning, you'll inevitably turn your gaze outward and take a look at the real world. You may not like what you see. You may start to question the way things work and look for ways the world could be improved. Great advances in social justice, in knowledge and technological achievements, only come about when people question the status quo and take measures to solve the problems.

DEVELOPING AN OBJECTIVE POINT OF VIEW

If you come forward and take the responsibility to change things, you need to be objective. There's a big difference between relating to things entirely in terms of how they affect you and being able to report them more or less as they would appear to anyone who might observe or know about them. If we tell about how a thing affected us, we are being **subjective**. If we tell about it as anyone might see it, we are being **objective**. Objectivity helps you to persuade other people and can gain you allies in making changes.

Consider these examples of what we mean:

Subjective:	Objective:
"That big, mean, ugly dog bit me."	*"I was playing with a dog, and unfortunately I began to play a little too roughly. The animal must have experienced some pain as I pulled on its tail and in self-defense reached out and nipped me on the hand."*
"My teacher is so unfair. She gave me a D on my essay."	*"My essay didn't meet the teacher's standards. I'll have to ask her more specifically how I could have done better."*

These examples might make a subjective approach seem childish, and an objective approach more adult and thoughtful. However, either point of view can be adult and thoughtful. Most great art, for example, is an exploration or development of a subjective point of view.

But in the process of learning and developing we have to learn to shift from seeing the world as being centered only around us to seeing it in such a way that many people can agree on what it means. That allows us to communicate effectively and persuasively with others.

_____

_____

_____

_____

_____

_____

ASKING QUESTIONS HAS MANY BENEFITS

As you improve your ability be an active learner, you'll also discover the value and importance of your differences from the rest of your group. People will begin to know you for your special talents and point of view.

If you've been in a situation where you felt you were being criticized more often than you were praised, perhaps it is a little difficult for you to understand this. But it's true that when people are praised for what they do right, they learn to value themselves more, and thus to value the things that set them apart from others. Many books on success, by the way, have titles like **Dare To Be Different**. So learn to respect and value your differences by noticing all the different ways in which you are successful.

If no one else is telling you what you do right, you may have to learn how to tell yourself. In other words, you're going to stop seeing yourself in terms of your inadequacies and start seeing your strengths. That way you'll begin making stronger contributions to all the groups of which you are a part. The more you emphasize your positive points, the more enjoyable and meaningful your life can become.

Try This ☞

Need some practice asking questions?

Here's a game you can play with a friend: Choose an object in the room. Take turns asking questions about it — all kinds of questions, no answers are necessary. This deceptively simple game can lead you in surprising directions. Does it stimulate your thinking in any interesting ways?

7
Patterns: Having Fun With Test-Taking

Test-taking can be one of the most awful things in life — or one of the most wonderful. In this chapter we'll try to give you the chance to make it as much fun for yourself as taking in a movie or a party. If you don't believe that, perhaps you can at least raise it to the level of enjoyment of a TV quiz show. The main tool we'll introduce you to is the fifth of the Basic Skills: Pattern Recognition. We'll look at many different kinds of patterns that can be helpful in test-taking, such as determining the main points of structure, distinguishing between content and process, building the vocabulary you need to understand the subject, core concepts, comparing and contrasting, getting yourself into the subject, and overlearning. We'll also work on improving your attitude, and preparing for the event itself.

Taking a test can be one of the most enjoyable activities in your life. Many people get more fun out of testing themselves and being tested than they do out of almost anything else.

Some people do it at carnivals where they test their strength at moving heavy objects, their skill at shooting targets, their ability to make beautiful arrangements of sand in bottles, and so on. Others go out for sports, where they constantly test their athletic ability and play hard for long hours. Still others like crossword puzzles, Rubic's Cubes, or other kinds of puzzles. Some people play chess or cards or video games. These are all different kinds of tests. They all involve combinations of knowledge and skill, plus a way of keeping track of your progress.

LEARNING TO DISLIKE TESTS IN SCHOOL

It's only in school that people dislike tests. This is strange. Why should anything so enjoyable in the world at large be so unpleasant in school? Tests in school should be as much fun as tests in a video arcade, a carnival, television quiz shows, or sports.

WHY STUDENTS SO OFTEN HATE TESTS

Most of us don't like the kinds of tests we get in school because we don't think we're supposed to like them. Most of us have learned to regard tests as difficult, and unpleasant, even though if they were called something else we might enjoy them.

Of course it's not much fun to take a test on something you hate studying, particularly if you're not prepared. And it's not much fun to be told your whole future may depend on the outcome of a test on which you don't think you did well.

But wouldn't it be nice if we never had to face such problems again. Fortunately, there are ways to make your test-taking more successful. It's mainly a matter of learning a few rather simple techniques.

THE TWO BASIC CHALLENGES IN TEST-TAKING

There are two main things to deal with in taking tests. The first involves preparing yourself with enough information. The second involves your attitude.

No matter how good your attitude is, if you don't know much about the material you're being tested on, you probably won't do very well. On the other hand, if your attitude toward being tested is poor, you probably won't do your best with what you do know.

Let's first consider how to be sure you'll remember the information you need in order to be successful on the test.

In earlier chapters we've explored ways to prepare yourself to learn. These include finding the right goals, learning the principles of organizing things, becoming an active learner, getting feedback on how you're doing, finding out what needs to be done next, taking good notes, listening well, and solving problems.

Now, what do you do when you've studied the material in the book, taken lecture notes, and are ready to review everything for a test? This is a good time to consider the fifth of the Five Basic Skills: pattern recognition.

PATTERN POWER

Recognizing patterns enables you to turn a large amount of information into a smaller amount that's easier to think about. It's a sort of magic trick, like turning a stick into a bouquet of flowers. Let's perform one of these magic tricks right now, so you can see how easy it is to be a magician of the mind.

First look at this word: XZYP. Now look at this word: STOP. The word XZYP is confusing because you probably don't recognize it as a pattern. It has four separate letters, and it's hard to remember what order they come in. The word STOP is easy to remember. It, too, has four letters, but you see it as a single word because the pattern of the letters is meaningful to you. You can therefore think of the four letters as one word. In this way, once you learn the pattern in the word STOP, you can understand four times as much information with the same amount of effort as it took before you learned the pattern.

PATTERNS ARE EVERYWHERE

Think of sound. We are surrounded by sounds: natural, noisy, disorganized. Arrange them in pleasing patterns of tone and rhythm and music is created.

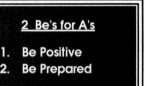

2 Be's for A's

1. Be Positive
2. Be Prepared

Key Word

Patterns can be used to help organize what we know and what we see. Did you know that confusion itself is organized? This is a very recent scientific discovery that may amuse you. Almost any wild, confusing chaos turns into rather well organized patterns if you look at it from the right point of view.

If that is true of wild confusion, how much more true it is of music and language and numbers. Once we start to see the patterns in what we observe, we can understand many things we otherwise might miss.

Think about the patterns in activities you are involved in everyday. There's a pattern in baseball or football which is described partly by the rules and partly by effective ways of playing the games. There's a pattern in a rap or a song described partly by the rhythm and partly by the rhymes. There's a pattern in making new friends: the set of steps we go through to get acquainted, learn to trust one another and gradually build a relationship.

When you start looking for patterns in the things you're studying, you'll find your studies will get more interesting and also easier. Then you'll no longer be just memorizing isolated facts, you'll be understanding and interpreting them as well, perhaps making up your own theories about how things work or how they fit together. You'll really be thinking.

In fact, the famous geniuses who invent machines or write books or compose music are people who are very good at performing magic tricks with patterns. But it's really not hard — you can learn to do it too.

HOW TO DISCOVER USEFUL PATTERNS

We're going to teach you several ways to organize your subject matter before a test. These different approaches will help you to find patterns within the subject. You'll find some approaches are more suited to particular subjects or more suited to your way of thinking. You may want to use more than one approach. They are all going to help you to study better.

DETERMINING THE MAIN POINTS OF STRUCTURE

When you begin to study, you should first determine the structure of the subject. Think of the material as having two basic parts: the structure of the subject — you could call this the big picture and secondly, the details within the big picture.

Perhaps you can see that in the design of this chapter we've been dividing up the subject. First we said that there are two things that are important in test-taking: what you know, and your attitude. Then we said that within the general area of what you know, you should look for patterns, and that there are several different methods for finding the patterns. Then we plunged into the first of these approaches which divides subject matter into the structure and the details. We've been structuring the subject of test-taking to give you an overview, the big picture.

You could take this structure and make a diagram of it like this:

Here's another example: The United States consists of 50 states, grouped into large regions and within each state there are cities and counties. The cities are where the population and commercial activity are concentrated.

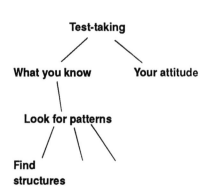

Create a diagram of this
information about U.S.
geography:

United States

The counties are the larger sections of land, some of which contain large cities, but many of which have very little population or commercial activity.

In saying this much about our country, we've given a general idea of how things are organized — the structure. It will now be possible to fill in details: to learn the names of the regions and states and their capital cities, and learn the general characteristics of each group, to learn what makes each state and city unique, and so on. By having an overall structure in mind, we know where to put details as we gather them.

When it comes to reviewing for a test, decide what general divisions you can make in the subject. Then group the facts you have to learn into clusters that can be put somewhere in the overall structure. Keep making your structures within structures more detailed as you fill in information.

How to Look for the Structure

Here are some questions to ask yourself to get thinking:

What are the different categories of facts or concepts?

How are the different categories related to one another?

Which can be grouped together?

Are some categories within other categories?

Can I arrange these categories in a framework diagram or map?

PRETEND YOUR SUBJECT IS A FOREIGN LANGUAGE

In many ways you can think of the subject you are studying as a foreign language. In language learning, vocabulary and grammar are the two most important things you have to learn. You have to know (a) what words mean, and (b) how to put them together to make sentences. The structure of your subject is like the grammar of a language.

LEARNING THE KEY TERMS

Now you can focus on the vocabulary of your subject by making lists of key terms and going over them until they're clear. The number of key terms might be fewer than ten, or more than two thousand. These are the details of your subject. You can fit them into your structure and learn what they mean.

Learn the most general key terms first, then the specific examples that follow from them. Then go to the next level of importance and decide which terms belong here. Again, study the relationships between these. That's the grammar: the way the key terms fit together to create concepts. For example; in studying the geography of the United States you might first want to study the term state, and make a list of all the states, then you may choose one state and make a list of the important characteristics of that state, then you may choose a certain characteristic, like agriculture in that state and study that.

To make sure you understand the key terms, define them in two different ways. First, write down a verbal description of each term. Second, draw a picture or diagram representing the concept behind the term.

Drawing the picture is important because too often we memorize definitions without actually understanding what they mean. But you can't draw a picture of something until you know what it is. If you're having trouble drawing a picture of a particular definition, think about the definition until you understand it — then you'll be able to draw it.

COMPARING AND CONTRASTING

Another way to deepen your understanding of key terms is to explore the similarities and differences between them. Compare and contrast the main ideas in the subject you are studying. If you're studying types of literature, make sure you can list many similarities and differences between poems and short stories, or between the drama and the novel. In literature you'll also want to look for repeated patterns in the behavior of characters or in plots. If you are studying biology, compare and contrast fins, wings and legs, and so on. The more similarities and differences you can spell out in this way, the better you will understand each concept. And the better you'll become at finding patterns.

ONCE AGAIN, APPLY WHAT YOU'VE LEARNED

So let's explore an example of how you might apply this method. You might take the subject of the human body, and write down a list of key terms. These can include things like head, skeleton, circulatory system, hair, and so on.

Next create a structure of the subject. Make a diagram or group your lists. Ask yourself, "which of these terms are most important, and which might be studied after learning the main terms?" For example, you'd normally study the term skeleton first and then thigh bone.

Now represent all the relationships and meanings in a sketch of the human body which includes not only the body parts but some way of representing what they do and what is important about them.

Don't worry about your drawing skills. What matters is that when you finish this method of review, you will have a very clear picture *in your mind* of what the parts of the body are and what they do.

DISTINGUISHING BETWEEN CONTENT AND PROCESS

As you're studying, it's important to understand the difference between content and process. Some of your key terms will be content and some will be processes. **Content** consists of the specific items of information you are learning. If the subject for study is the United States, the content can include the states, the cities, the geographical areas, the commercial enterprises, the laws, the characteristics of the people, and other things that can be named and dealt with as if they were more or less unchanging.

Process includes historical events and trends, such as the rise of industrialism, or the movement of the population into the cities, or changes in the role of the United States as a world power, or the electoral process, or the legal system. There are many other processes that are continually changing and are producing change.

For example, when we think of New York City in terms of content, we think of things that are likely to be there for long periods of time, such as the Empire State Building, Broadway, Madison Avenue, Harlem, the Brooklyn Bridge, and other such landmarks.

But when we think of New York City's political system, which can be considered process, we think of continual change: new candidates for office who may or may not be elected, political issues that are hot for a while and may disappear later, campaign slogans, corruption, voter blocs, conventions, and many other events that are seldom the same from one week or year to the next.

By dividing your subject into content and process, you can identify lists of things you have to remember. For the subject of anatomy, a content list might include the bones, muscles, systems, and reactions found in the human body — things you can identify by pointing to a picture, diagram, or chart.

A process list might include how the blood circulates, what happens when someone drinks too much alcohol, how a broken bone is repaired, how the body adjusts to nerve damage, and other continually changing interactions.

Check for more information:
  Diagrams of structure — p. 63
  Mind Maps — p. 68
  Memory devices — Chapter 8
  Flow charts — p. 34
  Stories — p. 80, p. 91

Often the best way to keep track of content is to make lists, diagrams of the structure, mind maps, or memory devices. The best way to keep track of process is to make flow charts, stories, or models. Prepare your own story and visual aids and your subject material will really sink in.

DEALING WITH CONTENT AND PROCESS ON TESTS

When a test is concerned with content, you'll often be asked for precise information, such as the name of a particular bone, the three main parts of the governmental system of checks and balances, the meaning of a quotation from *Romeo and Juliet*, or the formula for the area of a circle.

When you're tested on process, you'll probably be asked to think something through and describe it. You're more likely to have to write an essay than to give a short answer by filling in the blanks or multiple choice.

CORE CONCEPTS

Now we're going to give you a secret weapon for improving your studies — one very few people have ever used, but which could make a big difference in what you can accomplish once you have learned to use it. It's another kind of pattern recognition of the most basic ideas in human thinking, which we are going to call core concepts. They are concepts that will crop up in many different areas and subjects.

If you understand these ideas well enough, they can help you understand all at once many different things that don't at first seem to have much to do with each other. If you have thought carefully about several of these core concepts, you can apply them in a variety of subject areas in order to help you understand more quickly how the subject is organized.

Let's take one basic idea, *balance*, and see how it can be used to make sense out of things that might otherwise be confusing. When, long ago, you stood on two legs and began to walk, you had to balance yourself. That was difficult at first, but became easier with practice. Then maybe you learned to ride a bike and that, too, got easier with practice. How good are you at walking tight ropes, though? Tight rope walkers are people who have developed their sense of balance more than most of us.

Now take this idea of balance and apply it to some things other than walking. Did you ever think of the equal sign in a math equation as being like a balancing act? Each side of the equation has to balance the other side, just as you balance your body when you stand up. Similarly, in a sentence the subject and predicate must balance with one another.

When we study nutrition, we learn about a balanced diet. When we study government we learn about the balance of powers, and when we study international relations we learn about the balance of trade. If you like psychology, you're probably interested in how one develops a well balanced personality. In law there's the question of the balance of justice so everyone can get a fair deal. If you like to sell things, you know that there has to be a balance between the price you charge and the value of what you're selling.

We might go on giving hundreds and indeed thousands of examples of balance in all different subject areas, but the point is we are beginning to see a pattern here. This pattern can help us understand many things that might be confusing if we didn't think about how balance shows relationships among them.

SOME OTHER CORE CONCEPTS

Now let's look at some other concepts besides balance: Sequence is another of these concepts. We've already talked about it quite a bit in this book, but in any subject you can look for important sequences. In math, one sequence is the numbers one to infinity. Another is the order in which certain operations must be performed. Another is the movement from the statement of the problem to the solution. In literature an important sequence is from the exposition of a story through the climax to the final resolution.

Another core concept is structure. It tells you how things are built up so they hold together. There's the bone structure in your body, the network structure of a telephone system, the structure of relationships that holds a family together, or the molecular structure of a chemical compound.

Another core concept is system. A system is anything whose parts fit together so if you change something about one of them, the others are affected in some way. For example, in the weather system if there's no water on the ground to evaporate, clouds will not form in the sky, and it will not rain. So if any aspect of the weather system is changed, the others will be affected as well.

Can you think of some other core concepts?

THINKING WITH CORE CONCEPTS

If you come across a concept that you don't understand, ask yourself if you've seen the word or concept used someplace else, perhaps in another subject area. Understanding the concept in one context will help you understand it in other places. Take balance, for example: if you're having trouble understanding balance in a chemical equation, it might help you to compare it with balancing a checkbook, or balancing on a see-saw.

See if you can give examples of these other core concepts: opposition, exchange, movement, quality, function, feedback, change, similarity, communication, divergent, model, identity, forward, disruption, delay, list, subject, control, territory, process, context, event, beginning, form, size, quantity.

ENTER MIND MAPPING

Get a Map of the overview.

Now we're ready to introduce what may turn out to be the most valuable tool in this whole book. It's usually called Mind Mapping. It's somewhat like related techniques that have been called "concept mapping" or "webbing."

Mind mapping is a way of diagramming or picturing all the different distinctions we've been exploring above. It's a way of visually representing relationships that could make study much easier for you.

The reason Mind Maps work so well is that we do not think in little pieces of ideas, we think in ideas in relationship to each other. So if we have a system for putting something down on paper that shows all the important connections and relationships with other things or ideas, then it's easy to understand and remember it.

NO SPECIAL EQUIPMENT REQUIRED

To Mind Map all you need is a few sheets of blank paper. Draw a circle in the center of one of them, and put in it the main idea of what you are studying. Then, pretending it's the hub of a wheel, draw spokes out from it with supporting ideas. Each of these spokes can have lines coming out of it with ideas supporting the supporting idea. Thus you can begin to group ideas so they reveal their relationships to each other.

Your Mind Map reflects your understanding, not someone else's, and therefore it may not look like a Mind Map drawn by someone else in your class based on the same material. Each will be different, and each will reflect the understanding of the person who drew it.

Of course you can always revise your Mind Map later, or you can put it into outline form. But making it in the first place is what is most important, because you're keeping a visual record of your thinking.

If you're artistically inclined, you can make the Mind Map elaborate, using lots of colors and pictures. Otherwise, if you prefer, you may keep it quite simple. Either way it can be a valuable tool to help you understand the material you're learning.

When it comes to studying for a test, there's probably no better way than making a Mind Map of the material you're studying, or going over Mind Maps you made earlier of that same material. This will help you see the patterns and relationships you need to understand in order to do well on the test.

ROSCOE GIVES IT A TRY

Roscoe's teacher asked him to make drawings to represent ideas in a sentence. Roscoe thought this meant drawing a picture representing each word in the sentence, and he was stuck because he thought he had to draw a picture for "the". This he did not know how to do.

Roscoe's teacher explained that it was not necessary, or even a good idea, to try to draw everything. It was important to draw something that would remind Roscoe of the idea being explored by the sentence, but NOT the exact words. For example, if we were to try to draw a picture of the idea of this sentence, we might show a picture of a stick figure with a question mark over its head making a drawing of a stick figure with a question mark over its head. If that doesn't sound like the best way to represent the previous sentence with a drawing, see if you can think of a better idea.

Not all ideas lend themselves to being expressed by pictures of things. Some of them, like the idea of confusion, or the idea of development, suggest doodles that do not really represent anything, but instead give the feeling that lies behind the word. If you made doodles like these, they would mean something to you, but not necessarily to anyone else.

Once Roscoe understood the way he was to draw pictures of ideas, he was able to start making these pictures and showing relationships among them similar to those in the Mind Map at the beginning of this book. He became so fascinated with the process that when it became time to do his homework that night, he didn't want to stop. He spent many hours Mind Mapping the material in his text book. He went well beyond the chapter assigned, and then even went back and Mind Mapped material he had studied earlier.

Roscoe really enjoyed finding his own way to express these new things he was learning. And afterwards, he found he could both remember and understand the material in the chapters much, much better than before.

USE IT FOR GETTING THINGS INTO— OR OUT OF — YOUR MIND

So far we've been talking about using Mind Mapping mainly for organizing and remembering things that are outside you: information found in books or learned in classes. But Mind Mapping is also a terrific tool for getting thoughts and ideas out of your head, on to paper where you can look at them, play with them, and develop them in new ways.

Suppose you want to plan a report or a project or even write a story. If you are like lots of people, it's often hard to know where to begin. Sometimes you're not even sure you're clear in your own mind about what you're trying to do. How do you start when you don't know where you're going?

That's where Mind Mapping can help. It's not like an outline where you have to know how every idea is related to every other idea pretty much before you can write down the number "1". Or like a writing assignment where you might be asked for an introduction, a middle, and a conclusion. Most of us don't think about things that way — though we can see the value of being able to express our ideas that way once we've thought them through.

THE RIGHT TOOL FOR YOUR WAY OF THINKING

Use Mind Maps to plan your writing assignments and other projects.

The beauty of Mind Mapping is that it is flexible, and it can be made up and constantly revised as you go along, and there's no one right way to do it. In fact, you can adapt it to the way you actually think. Mind mapping is something like thinking out loud. Except that it has the extra advantage that you can change what you've thought as you go along, and when you're finished with Mind Mapping (unlike with thinking out loud) you've got a record of what you've thought. And then your job of organizing it for any particular purpose can now be easily done.

So — getting back to that report or story — you might begin by jotting down words or phrases to remind yourself of ideas that seem important to you about your subject, or areas that you want to remember to cover. With a Mind Map, you don't have to make a list. Spreading them out allows you to see them easily, and begin to see relationships between them.

If you think you know the main idea you want to write or talk about, you could put it in the middle of the paper as a kind of a hub, a center. But it may be that the main idea only begins to become clear to you as you see the thoughts you've jotted down to get them out on the paper. Sometimes one of the ideas that seemed rather minor when you first jotted it down turns out to be the main thing you were driving at. So you could make that your new center, by circling it or highlighting it in some way — or perhaps by starting on a new sheet of paper. Whatever works best for you and keeps the process interesting and fun.

The openness and flexibility of a Mind Map allows you to make connections and move ideas and information around as you go along. You can cross things out, circle a note and attach it with a line to another part of the map, or just start a new map. So you don't have to worry about making mistakes.

The more you practice Mind Mapping, the easier and more useful it will become for you. Soon you will find yourself developing your own system or shorthand for jotting down notes in words or doodles, or perhaps a system of colors and connecting lines and symbols, or some combination of them. You will be seeing how **you** think — and you will be using your powers of thinking more quickly and efficiently to learn and do the things you want to do.

GETTING PERSONALLY INVOLVED

Get Emotional About The Subject

Finally, you'll understand the material better if you get involved personally. How do you **feel** about what you are studying? Again, suppose you are studying the human body. You come to the circulatory system. Does the sight of blood make you want to faint or throw up? Admit it. Then think about what it would be like if you could get in a boat and float through the blood stream of the human body like an explorer. Would this make you feel differently about blood?

Most people would get sick if they saw a broken bone sticking through someone's skin, but when you think about how the skeleton gives the body its basic shape and structure, that's a different feeling. Pretend you're a sculptor and want to know how all the parts of the body fit together so you can make a life-size model of a human being.

By bringing your personal reactions into your studies, you can make them all more memorable. Like the student who can remember the score for every World Series game ever played, or the one who knows all the words to all the hit songs, you'll be able to remember things surprisingly well after you become emotionally involved with them. Human beings just naturally remember things better when they feel strongly about them.

OVERLEARNING

Now we come to the idea of overlearning. That means going over the material enough so you're sure you know it, rather than going over it only enough so you think you know it. Memory devices are good tools for practicing overlearning. In the next chapter we'll teach you lots of tricks to help you develop a super memory.

THE IMPORTANCE OF GROUP STUDY

Preparing for an exam works better if you study in a group than all by yourself. The people in your study group can think of more ideas while working together and can stimulate each other's thinking. You can look for patterns together, do a group Mind Map with everybody participating. Every members' performance will improve.

So if you haven't already formed a study group, take a look at Chapter 11 and organize one in time to help you study for your next test.

PLANNING THE FINAL REVIEW

To plan your final review, determine how much material you're going to cover and how much time you have to cover it in. Block out a schedule allowing a fifteen-minute break after each hour of study. Then look over the materials you are going to study — text, notes, questions, outside readings and Mind Maps — and divide them according to your schedule.

Set goals.

Sequence.

If you have four different types of study material, to spend fifteen minutes with each during each hour of study. That way, your attention is constantly being shifted. One set of materials will refresh you from another set, making your study time more interesting and varied.

During the review time, make 3 x 5 inch cards with the key points from your notes and readings and go over them several times. This will help you overlearn the material, since it's easier to remember what you write than what you read.

EARLIER PREPARATION FOR THE FINAL REVIEW

You will find it's a good idea to set up a regular review process from the beginning of a course. At the end of your study period for a particular subject, set aside time to relate the new material to material you've already studied. Remind yourself of the overview of the subject and fit the newly-acquired details into it. Spend a certain amount of time reviewing old material for every hour spent learning new material.

Find out how you're doing.

IMPROVING YOUR ATTITUDE ABOUT TEST-TAKING

Now let's consider attitudes that can either help you take a test more effectively or get in your way.

It's hard to do well at something if you (a) believe you can't or (b) have a lot of negative emotions related to it. Therefore, the best spirit in which to take a test is one of peaceful, calm relaxation. You might do twice as well on a test if you're relaxed.

CAN NERVOUSNESS HELP YOU?

Look at it this way. There's no way being nervous about a test can improve your performance. Whatever the state of your knowledge when you walk into an exam, you can't improve it by worrying. Either you know the material or you don't. Being nervous, however, can help you *forget* the material — and lower your grade.

The more tense and anxious you are, the more energy you drain away from your performance on the test. And, as you probably know, even in a physically stressful situation like a fall, if you tense up you're much more likely to get hurt. The best frame of mind is like that of athletes and performers who are excited, want to do their best, and know that they will enjoy themselves — especially when they are well prepared.

But if you're like most people, getting to that frame of mind before taking a test may be more an ideal than something real for you. You've been learning a lot of tools that will make it easier for you to prepare for tests. But let's take a look at what else might be be blocking your path to success.

ATTITUDES ABOUT TESTS THAT CAN BE HURTFUL

Before you take another test, you can do yourself a world of good by taking a close look at your attitude toward tests. Here's an exercise that can help you.

Possibly your present attitude could be summarized like this:
1) *Tests are terrible experiences.*
2) *I can't think well during tests.*
3) *I'm pretty sure I'll forget what I know while I'm taking tests.*
4) *I'd do well in school if it weren't for tests.*
5) *I can succeed on a test only if I stay up the night before, cramming.*
6) *I can't put what I know into words.*
7) *I can't write well enough to please the teacher.*

Look over these statements and see if any of them are true of you. Then copy them down, changing them to fit you more precisely. Add any other statements that describe your present attitude toward test-taking.

Here are some other attitudes that keep me from performing well on tests:

_____

_____

_____

CREATING POSITIVE BELIEFS FOR YOURSELF

Your next job is to revise these statements to reflect not what you believe now, but what you would like to believe about yourself in the future.

Here's how they might read in their new forms:

1) Tests are very enjoyable, relaxed, fun experiences, during which I always have a chance to show off how brilliant I am.

2) I think extremely well during tests.

3) I'll remember everything I studied while I'm taking tests. And I'll also put the information together in inspired new ways that help me shine.

4) I do so well in school partly because I perform so brilliantly on tests.

5) I am always fully prepared for a test, because I keep the material in mind all the time.

6) I'm especially good at putting what I know into words.

7) Every time I take a test, my writing gets better.

DON'T JUST REVISE — ADVERTISE!

Making the revised list is one thing; believing it is another. You may doubt that you can adopt these new attitudes. But you can. How do you think you got your old attitudes? You convinced yourself they were true. It's probably going to take some convincing until you adopt these new attitudes.

Learning the skills that will make you succeed will give you confidence and put your doubts to rest. And in the meantime, here's a suggestion you might try:

Make a poster for each statement and hang it on your wall to remind yourself of what you'd like to believe. Use color in your posters, and make them as artistic as you can. Whenever someone visits your room, show off the posters and explain what they're for.

FIXING THE NEW ATTITUDES IN YOUR MIND

While dropping off to sleep each night, mentally review the new statements that express what you'd like to believe about test-taking. Do the same review when you awaken in the morning.

From time to time during the day, review the statements. An excellent time to do this is while you're taking a walk. Chant or rap the statements, walking in rhythm to the words as they pass through your mind.

Remember, instilling in yourself a positive attitude is important to your successs. Be sure to surround yourself with others who are motivated to succeed and supportive of your top performance, as well as their own, so mutual positive attitudes will speed you toward your goal more rapidly and effectively.

If you have a tape recorder, record these statements and play them back

> **Put It On
> A Poster**

at least once a day while listening to your favorite music. This won't interfere with your enjoyment of the music. Many people find this technique is particularly effective if you turn up the music enough to drown out your tape. That way, your inner mind will hear the messages and respond to them better.

BE EARLY FOR THE GRAND EVENT

Breathe — for your brain.

On the day of a test, walk into the test room early. Calmly take your seat and breathe deeply several times. Your brain demands oxygen to think. Although your brain weighs less than three pounds, it uses a large part of the oxygen you breathe. You might also want to close your eyes and suggest to yourself that this is a test you will do well on. Then let go of any negative feelings about the test and have fun with it.

PACING THE TEST

Begin by reading the test instructions a couple of times. Often students fail to read instructions and thus make a mistake they otherwise would not have made. Then look over the whole test (or as much of it as you're allowed to see at the moment) and get an idea of what it covers. Then pick out the parts you know best. Do those parts first.

The parts you don't think you know will come to you while you work on what you do know. You'll remember them more easily if you know what answers you're looking for, and that's what you'll accomplish by looking over the whole test at the beginning. While you're doing the part you know, your inner mind will be working on the part you don't know, jogging hidden memories, figuring out possible approaches, and so on.

While you're working on the test, you might not remember material from the class or from your recent studying, but you might remember something about the subject from other experiences you've had. Or perhaps you can figure out an answer just by using logic.

As you're taking the test, have a clock in your head that tells you how much time you have to spend on each part. Then pace yourself, keeping a little ahead of the clock.

With time, you'll discover how much fun it can be to take tests. Then you'll be able to go through the rest of your education eagerly looking forward to what many other students may still be afraid of. You'll have good reason to be proud of yourself when that happens.

Try This 👉

Need some practice looking for patterns?

Play this game with a friend: What does that shadow remind you of? Take turns looking for familiar shapes or pictures in clouds and shadows. See if your friend can recognize the shape as well.

8

Developing A Super Memory

In this chapter we'll explore your memory — how it works, and how it can work better. You'll get some ideas about why forgetting occurs, and some hints about how to make it occur less frequently when you want to remember something. Memory is a matter partly of having the right kinds of tricks to lock something in so you can get it back when you want it, and partly of having a positive emotional attitude toward what you're learning. Using these memory tricks can be fun. So relax and enjoy, remembering what you learn in this chapter.

One of the best ways to become a better student is to utilize your memory.

YOUR MEMORY IS ALREADY PERFECT

You already have a perfect memory. You might have to improve your **access** to your memory, but your memory itself is perfect. Many medical researchers believe that everything that happens to you is permanently recorded in your memory and could be brought back by the surgical probing of your brain.

THEN WHY DO WE FORGET?

Your perfect memory is in your head just waiting for you to tap it. The trick is learning how. Your mind also has the capacity to forget, so you remember only things you believe are useful at the moment. Your brain is intelligent enough to cause you to forget anything that has one or more of the following characteristics:

1) It is too disturbing.

2) It is boring.

3) It is not different enough from other things that have happened.

4) It isn't fun, and therefore deep in your heart you'd like to forget it.

5) Remembering it would contradict your impression that you have a terrible memory.

6) It doesn't fit in with what you wish you were doing at the moment.

7) You think the people around you would think you were weird if you could remember it.

8) Zillions of other reasons your mind can think of to block the memory from your consciousness.

If none of these reasons were in your way, you'd be able to recall just about anything that ever happened to you — provided you were aware of it with some part of your mind when it happened.

THE LIMITATIONS OF PERFECT MEMORIES

A perfect memory, however, isn't much use if it is just a series of recalled events. There was once a man in Russia who had conscious recall of everything that ever happened to him. Asked what he had eaten for breakfast on a day twenty or so years earlier, he could describe the breakfast exactly.

But he usually had to go back and mentally review the process of getting up in the morning on that day and preparing for breakfast.

In other words, everything was in his memory in chronological order, but he couldn't do much that was useful to him with all the memories. He couldn't think with them or organize them in any fruitful way. They were just there to be unrolled like the reels of a movie.

WHAT A GOOD MEMORY SHOULD BE ABLE TO DO

That's not the kind of recall you want. You want to be able to go anywhere in your memory and get what you need at the moment. To do this, you'll need to work on your memory much as you might go into a book store where all the books are scattered around and organize them so the customers can find what they're looking for.

In this chapter we'll give you a few techniques to help you do that.

TECHNIQUE NUMBER ONE: **Learn from the general to the specific**. Little details are not much use by themselves. They need to be tied together by a larger structure. It's easier to remember the little things if you've already learned the big things. So memorize the outline for the course before you memorize any of the specifics.

TECHNIQUE NUMBER TWO: **Make it meaningful**. Make connections between the material you're studying and things, people, ideas, or goals that are of value to you. All meaning has to be personal. If the material doesn't fit into your personal set of meanings, then as far as you're concerned, it has no meaning.

Most of us are conditioned to think of memory as mechanical — that we memorize in order to parrot back without necessarily thinking about it. This is called "rote learning." So the idea of giving meaning to what we are learning may meet with resistance at first. But in the end, it makes studying and learning more fun, and remembering easier.

TECHNIQUE NUMBER THREE: **Create Associations**. The way to remember something is to associate it with something else that is already familiar to you. For example, if you meet a woman whose name is Betsy

You remember the things that matter to you.

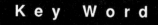

K e y   W o r d

Stanforth, you can remember her name more easily if you build a set of associations with it. Perhaps you have previously known a Betsy who looks like her — find similar facial features and concentrate on mentally seeing the name "Betsy" inscribed in her hair.

SEE your associations

Or you might think of Betsy Ross and visualize an American flag across her face or on her dress.

To get the last name, "Stanforth," see her standing forth. Perhaps she is standing in a line of Marines and a big, bellowing sergeant yells at her, "Betsy! Stand forth!" Whereupon she leaps out of the line giggling and waving an American flag.

You can remember any name, fact, or other bit of information by creating fantasies like this. However difficult it might be to create such a fantasy the first time you try it, it's worth spending the time, because you'll find soon enough that you can create such fantasies easily and quickly any time you want. It just takes a little practice.

TECHNIQUES INVOLVING YOUR BODY

The above three techniques are all forms of mental organization. Now let's move on to some techniques that get your body into the act.

TECHNIQUE NUMBER FOUR: **Learn it once actively**. It's much easier to learn something if your whole body is actively engaged. You'll remember the thing better if you're walking when you first try to memorize it than if

HOW TO REMEMBER TELEPHONE NUMBERS

The same process of associations will work with numbers. One way is to create a set of relationships within the number itself. Here's an example. If you have to remember the phone number 356-8384, do something like this:

Notice the exchange — 356. It could be 3456, but the four is missing. It has been stolen and put at the end of the number. So mentally see the 3 reaching around to the end and putting in the 4.

Now for the rest of the number. You already know it ends with 4. Double the 4 to get the 8. It's natural to double the 4, because the 8 occurs twice. The other number you need, between the two 8's, can be obtained by stealing the 3 from

the front. That's a fair exchange, since you already did it the other way.

So for the second number in each group you borrow the outside number from the other group. Except that in one case you're getting rid of the second number in the natural sequence, whereas in the other case you're putting in the needed second number.

This may seem complicated, but it will take you far less time to work out all these relationships and go over them several times than it will to repeat the number enough times so you won't forget it. Plus, it's more interesting.

In order to remember that 356-8384 is the telephone number of Betsy Stanforth, notice that the 4 in 3456 has to stand forth from

the first group and retreat to the end of the second, and the 3 in 8384 also has to stand forth and be used again at the front of the first group.

Now you can connect the phone number and the name with the same memory trick you used to remember the name in the first place. And if this seems like the long way around a simple problem, don't worry. With a little practice you will be doing it very quickly, in much less time than it takes to explain it.

Tricks like this always work better if you invent them yourself than if you read about them, or if someone else thinks them up for you. The very act of creating such a trick helps plant the memory more firmly.

you're lying down. You'll also remember it better if you can declaim it out loud like a ham actor than if you keep it inside.

So even if it seems a little awkward at first, give it a try. Sit up, or stand up. Walk around or pace. Shout out the words. Use your hands to make pictures in the air. March in rhythm while chanting the key words.

TECHNIQUE NUMBER FIVE: **Visualize relationships**. By making the left and right halves of your brain work together, you'll remember much better. When you've expressed the ideas in words, you've put them into the left hemisphere of your brain, which handles language, sequential ideas, and mathematical concepts. If you then create visual and sound images, you can get the material anchored in your right hemisphere as well. Some ways to do this include making Mind Maps, drawing cartoons or making up songs or raps. Turning abstract ideas into concrete actions also helps.

TECHNIQUE NUMBER SIX: **Recite and repeat**. Reciting words aloud makes them more memorable. This combines the sensation in the throat with hearing. Adding emotion to the recitation increases the memorability, and adding other body movements, such as clapping, increases it even more.

STRIVING FOR CLARITY

These last three techniques focused on getting the body involved. Now let's consider some techniques that help make the material clearer, so it can be remembered more easily.

TECHNIQUE NUMBER SEVEN: **Create the study area that's best for you**. Some people prefer bright light; others would rather have the light dim. Some prefer the absence of all interfering noise; others study better with the radio blaring. Some prefer to get up and move around frequently; others want to hole up in a place where there is no temptation to move. Some prefer to eat while they study; others would find that a distraction. Some study best with a friend on the telephone. Some like to interweave their study with other activities, such as cooking a meal or painting a picture.

Discover the kind of study place that best fits your learning style.

Each person has a set of best conditions for studying, which depend on their particular personalities. But most people don't take the trouble to find out what their best conditions might be. You can discover yours by experimenting until you've zeroed in on the most important things that help focus your thinking. You'll be getting a lot of help with this in Chapter 10.

TECHNIQUE NUMBER EIGHT: **Get new perspectives**. When you have the subject well in hand from your textbook, lecture notes, and other study aids that come with the course, seek out additional points of view and perspectives on the material. You'll understand and remember it better when you begin to see it as part of a dialogue in which people are arguing about something. There probably isn't any subject or bit of academic information that somebody doesn't want to argue about, including the sum of 2 and 2.

When you find yourself in a stimulating argument about the subject you're studying, it will seem more interesting, more understandable, and more memorable.

TECHNIQUE NUMBER NINE: **Build your own philosophy**. Almost all course work assumes a passive learner — most texts, most teachers, and most other students assume you could not possibly contribute anything new to that subject.

Yet everyone who has made a contribution to progress in any field — Albert Einstein, Florence Nightingale, Duke Ellington, William Shakespeare, or the Marx Brothers — was once a beginner like you, knowing no more than you do now. All these people were probably treated as passive learners by someone, but they rose above it.

You can too. Develop your own theories about the material. Try them out in conversations and discussions. If you find others getting disgusted with your ideas, there is probably something worth thinking about in them. Most new ideas are treated with contempt when first presented to a friend, a teacher, or the public. It is often true that the better the idea, the more contempt it arouses when it's first heard.

Explore your own point of view.

But don't get yourself into the position of failing the course because you're thinking too much and too well. Like Galileo, who agreed to renounce his theories so he wouldn't be killed, back off from yours if you need to pass the course.

But do indulge your thinking powers in speculation about how things might be different. Such speculations can sometimes lead to important insights. For example, in geometry you learned (or will learn) that the shortest distance between two points is a straight line and that only one straight line can connect two points. But what appears to be common sense, accepted by everybody, is not necessarily the last word on the subject. (It happens that non-Euclidean geometry, which describes the universe, contradicts these basic principles.)

MORE GENERAL PRINCIPLES FOR EFFECTIVE STUDY

Now here are some general principles that may help you organize your study time and technique.

TECHNIQUE NUMBER TEN: **Punctuate your day with learning**. Break up your study time and distribute it through the day, mingling it with other activities. That will keep you from getting exhausted from too much study at one time, and it will help you work the material over in your mind while doing something else. Studying this way can greatly increase the payoff you get per hour of study time.

If you spend a significant amount of time each day in public transportation or a car and can have a portable tape player, use this opportunity to augment your studying. Make interesting tapes about the material. You can tape many things, such as lists of items you wish to review, lectures from the radio or the library related to the subject you are studying, or memory devices to help you remember the key points. Play the tapes while you're traveling.

TECHNIQUE NUMBER ELEVEN: **Remember something else**. When you are stuck and can't remember something you know you know, remember something else that's related. This will jog your memory, since similar things or ideas seem to be stored close together in the brain.

It's like looking for something you've lost by remembering the last place you saw it. By thinking about things related to the missing piece, you'll jog your memory. Practice with this technique can make a big difference to your ability to get memories back when you need them.

TECHNIQUE NUMBER TWELVE: **Clean up your language**. When something's on the tip of your tongue, but you can't get it at the moment, don't say "I've forgotten," or "I can't remember." Phrases like these instruct your subconscious to have trouble remembering things. Instead say, "It will come to me," "I'll remember it soon," "Give me a minute and I'll have it," or some such phrase.

These are statements that instruct your mind positively. You'll find that if you use positive words instead of negative ones in this way, your memory will improve a lot.

Similarly, tell yourself from time to time — particularly when you're going to sleep at night or waking up in the morning — "I have an excellent memory." Eventually, perhaps to your surprise, you will discover that it's getting better.

You'll also notice you can trust your mind to deliver what you need. You might be in the middle of a sentence and not know how you're going to finish it. Pause slightly, giving your mind a chance to give you the words, and then continue, watching to see what comes out. You'll be amazed at how often your mind will give you just what you need once you've learned to trust it.

TECHNIQUE NUMBER THIRTEEN: **Create a weird story**. The main ideas you're trying to learn can be translated into images. The images can be combined to make a story that's so strange, weird, and bizarre, you can't possibly forget it. Let's demonstrate with putting the nine planets in their order from the sun:

> *The MERCURY was going up because it was so hot. VENUS was sunning herself, but the thermometer broke and the mercury spilled all over her. This so upset her that she blew a hole right through the EARTH, which started spinning on its axis so fast that all the mountains fell down beneath the oceans. MARS, a great big candy bar in the sky, melted at this and dripped all over the earth, plugging up the hole and restoring order. JUPITER, King of the Gods, began throwing thunder bolts to stir things up again, but suddenly he slipped and SATURN (sat in), right on his anus (not URANUS, his anus), a big pile of Non-Edible Produce which was playing a TUNE (N.E.P. TUNE). Then he BLEW on the TOE he had stubbed (BLEW TOE = PLUTO).*

This kind of thing, of course, is awful nonsense, but if you make it up yourself you'll find it easy to remember.

Just for fun, right now, try to write out a list of the nine planets in order from the sun. If you can't, read the above paragraph again. You ought to have the planets permanently in your mind with less than five minutes of this kind of study.

Don't talk yourself out of a good memory

Can you write a weirder story than this?

Stories are great devices for remembering the sequences of things (like the order of the nine planets). They're also helpful when you need to understand and remember complicated processes and explanations of how things work. The next time you're studying a scientific principle, an historical trend, a mathematical theorem see if you can tell yourself an interesting story about it, something that brings it fully into your grasp.

The odder the story, the easier it is to remember -- especially when you make it up yourself.

TECHNIQUE NUMBER FOURTEEN: **Memory Pegs** are visual images that can be associated with numbers. They are especially helpful when you want to memorize a numbered list of facts and be able to recall the fact as well as its number or place in the list. First you attach (peg) visual images to the numbers, so that you have in mind a mental picture for each number from 1 to 10. Then you can associate them with images for the items on your list, and thus memorize the list easily.

Let's, for example, learn how to memorize the names of the first ten Presidents of the United States. To make it easier and more fun, the ten memory peg images we're going to use for the numbers 1 to 10 will have two simultaneous ways of being associated with the ten numbers. First, each image is based on what the number actually *looks like*. Second, each has in it a word that *rhymes* with the number. Here they are:

Draw a picture here of each of the ten Memory Pegs -- it will make them stick in your memory:

1. A maypole dance is lots of fun. (The number one looks like a maypole, and the word "fun" rhymes with "one".)

2. A swan is swimming in the zoo.

3. These puddles flow in from the sea.

4. The sail on this boat can soar.

5. The hook on which the fish arrive.

6. This golf club can do many tricks.

7. A cliff on which to stand near heaven.

8. An hour glass that's always late.

9. A ball high up on an incline.

10. One fat, one skinny, makes two men.

You might have fun thinking up a set of pegs that you would enjoy using, but for the moment stick with these to see how they work.

HANGING THE PRESIDENTS ON MEMORY PEGS

Now let's see how we would memorize a list of the first ten Presidents of the United States. Their names are Washington, Adams, Jefferson, Madison,

Monroe, Adams, Jackson, Van Buren, Harrison and Tyler.

The trick is to associate something about the President in a weird but catchy way with the appropriate number image. You want to make the association unusual, bizarre and fun. For example, it's easy to have **Washington** skipping around the **maypole**, but if you think of the maypole there's nothing in that association to make you think of Washington. But if you put the Maypole in the middle of the Delaware River and visualize Washington swimming around it, then it's easier to remember.

Similarly, you could have **Adams** riding the **swan**, but that won't distinguish him from anyone else. On the other hand, if the swan has a big Adams apple, then you can remember.

Jefferson might be skipping through the **puddles** along the beach, but he'll need something to remember him by. You can associate him with Monticello, the home in which he lived. To do that mount (Mont) a cello on his back and have him skipping through the puddles burdened with the cello. If that doesn't work for you, maybe you'd like to visualize the Jefferson Starship dive bombing the puddles.

Madison needs to be associated with the **sail**. Use his name as a pun. Think of him as someone's mad son. Visualize him clinging to the sail, his legs swinging in the air, his red face screwed up with anger, shouting terrible things.

Monroe has to be associated with the **hook** for catching fish. You can use the second part of his name to row a boat, and the first part sounds like "Mom", so picture Mom rowing a boat in order to catch fish.

Now that we've given you five of the Presidents this way, see if you can do the other five yourself. If you make good images, you'll probably remember them better than the five we gave you, because it's easier to remember images you make yourself than those that are taught to you — provided the images you make yourself are really good ones.

Create your own memorable image for each of these Presidents

6. *A golf club* — President John Quincy Adams

_____

7. *A cliff* — President Andrew Jackson

_____

8. *An hour glass* — President Martin Van Buren

_____

9. *A ball on an incline* — President William H. Harrison

_____

10. *A fat man and a skinny man* — President John Tyler

_____

This kind of trick is artificial, weird, far-fetched, and probably not what you would have thought of initially. But it works because it is so absurd.

Practice will make this easier.

You'll find that this kind of exercise stimulates your imagination — and even if it's a little slow going at first, it will get easier each time you try it.

ONWARD TOWARD A SUPER MEMORY

If you practice all these techniques and use them regularly, you'll find lots of easy ways to combine them to get even more startling results.

Perhaps right now you think you have the worst memory in the world. You might even think you're getting senile, even if you're not yet officially an adult. But take our word for it — practice these techniques enough and you'll soon be ready to get up in front of an audience and demonstrate how magical your super memory is.

What kind of information is the most difficult for you to remember?

Decide which of the 14 techniques would work best for this kind of memorizing. Then try it.

9

Using All Your Intelligences

A lot has been learned recently about the brain, and much of it gives us important clues about how to study better. In this chapter you'll get acquainted with the differences between the left and the right brain — and how they can work together better. You will see the way your brain developed in prehistoric times, and why fear paralyzes your thinking and warm, comfortable emotions help you remember things better.

Then we'll look at the way all the ideas in your thinking tend to relate to each other, how you can grow more parts to your brain just by thinking better, and finally how you can improve your intelligence. No, not your intelligence (you have more than one) — all seven of your intelligences. So if you'd like to know how the workings of your particular brain influence your grades in school, read on!

How do you know there's a universe out there? How do you know you aren't just a disembodied brain or computer sitting in some mad scientist's laboratory with information being fed to you the way it is when you go to the movies? Suppose you were part of a huge 3-D lifelike movie that fed all the different senses, not just sight and sound, and that lasted for a lifetime. How could you tell the difference between that and actual real experiences?

HOW DESCARTES DECIDED HE EXISTED

This problem was confronted several centuries ago by a philosopher named René Descartes. He questioned everything, saying that nothing in the world could be proved to be true, because you could always argue that something else **might** be true.

Descartes argued that there was only one way you could be sure you existed, only one thing you could be certain of. He said, "I think, therefore I am." By this he meant that if he looked at his own private thoughts, he could see a difference between them and everything else that appeared to have meaning and reality.

WHAT YOU CAN REALLY BE SURE OF

Anything you see or hear could be nothing more than an illusion. But your own thoughts are something you can be certain of. You know they are yours.

You know you exist because you think. If you think, other people must as well. In fact, all human beings probably think in many of the same ways.

We cannot prove that animals do not think. We cannot even prove that trees, flowers, rocks and clouds do not think. But we know they do not communicate with us about their thinking the way we communicate with each other. Human beings can show one another that they are thinking and how they are thinking. This is the most important difference between human beings and everything else in the world.

So, because we can communicate about our own thinking in ways that animals cannot, we are human beings. No other distinction between us and animals is so important.

HOW DO WE KNOW WHAT THINKING IS?

But what is thinking? Much of what we think is thinking is not thinking at all. Most of what passes through your mind is not thinking, but recycling. It's a stream of words and images that replay experiences from the past and draw your attention away from making new changes in your life.

What we think of as thinking happens only when there is something new in the mind that didn't come directly from previous experience. You are thinking when you are putting two or more ideas together for the first time.

For example, if I ask you what do love and a rose have in common and you tell me they are both beautiful and they can both cause pain, this would be an example of real thinking — if you have never heard this idea before. But if you have, it's just a rehashing of someone else's idea. The point is that most of the time we are rehashing other people's ideas, and we spend too little time thinking of original ones of our own.

Real thinking is not just recycling old thoughts.

So the question is how do we stop just recycling and start thinking?

THE THOUGHT GARBAGE RECYCLING CENTER

Let's look at some of the things we could call recycling:

"Bumpo made a face at me on the way to school today, so after school I'm going to ambush him in the park and hurt him really bad."

This is not thinking because it's a replay of the old, "you did something to me, so I'll get you back" idea that goes on all the time not just between humans but also between lots of animals.

How could we change this to thinking?

THINKING CAN BE FUN

It's a lot easier to get interested in thinking if you take something of personal interest to you — something which might be bothering you — and start thinking about it. For example, here's how you might think about the situation described above.

Bumpo made a face at me on the way to school today. I wonder why he did. Maybe he was mad at me. Maybe he was upset about something. Maybe he just likes to make faces at people.

How could I find out why he did?

I could ask him.

I could ask someone else what he usually does.

I could decide I don't care because I have better things to think about.

This is thinking, because it explores several different reasons why this situation might have happened, and several different ways of dealing with it.

HOW TO KNOW WHEN YOU'RE THINKING

If you can think about a problem and arrive at a new solution, one you've never tried before, then you're thinking. If you just go on doing the same old stuff day after day and year after year, you're not thinking. And if you're not thinking, you're not acting like a real human being. You're not doing the sort of thing humans are born to do.

In recent years there has been a lot of good information to help us understand how we think and how we can improve our thinking on our own — either by ourselves or with a little help from our friends. There are five models we can use to think about how we think. These are models of the human brain.

FIVE NEW WAYS OF UNDERSTANDING THE BRAIN

The study of the brain is called **neuroscience**. It is a fascinating field of study, still full of so many exciting mysteries that our brain has been called the final frontier of science. By studying the brain from every possible point of view, neuroscientists have come up with various theories about how our brains work. These theories can be most easily understood through the use of models, which help us see the theories in action.

In the last several years the study of the brain has led to at least five new models of the brain, new ways to understand how people organize their thought processes. These include the **split brain**, the **triune brain**, the **whole picture brain**, the **self-growing brain** and the **seven intelligences**. Each of these models give us some fascinating clues about how our thought processes are organized. And we can use these clues to make better thinking possible.

HOW YOUR TWO SIDES TALK TO EACH OTHER

The first idea is that just as you have two hands, two eyes, and two legs, you also have two brains. The pink bundle of billions of nerve cells that sits in the top part of your head is divided in two, like an apple cut in half. Its left and right sides are joined by a small bundle of nerves that allows these two largely independent brains to talk to each other.

WHAT THE LEFT BRAIN DOES

The left brain, it has been found, likes to do the kinds of things most of us are expected to do in school. It likes to read, to write, to discuss ideas,

You're Well Equipped To Do Your Own Thinking

and to use words and logic in all sorts of ways. It likes to organize everything in sequence. In other words, it likes to make lists of things that go in order.

People whose thinking is strongly effected by their left brain often like to establish routines for themselves. They may, for example, like to get up every morning at the same time, and do the same general things at the same general times. Or if they take a vacation, they may like it to be at the same time and place each year.

If these are things you like to do, you are probably good at using your left brain.

_____

_____

_____

Here are some 'left-brain activities' I like to do.

ENTER THE RIGHT BRAIN

The right brain likes to deal with feelings. It likes to get an overview of things. It likes music and art. It likes to make maps and models of things and does not care too much about the order in which they occur.

Right brain people like to hang loose. They might lie around in bed one morning and get up early the next. From day to day they like things to be different. They like surprises. They like to see what will happen next and react to that, rather than force themselves to follow a schedule.

If you would rather do these kinds of things, you are probably good at using your right brain.

_____

_____

_____

Here are some 'right-brain activities' I like to do.

WHOLE-BRAINED PEOPLE

Of course no one is exclusively left- or right-brained. But some people seem to be better at using both sides of their brains together. We call these whole-brained people. These people are good at using words and logic. They're good at making lists of things and putting things in order.

But they also like to be spontaneous, think about feelings, and get the whole picture. And they like music and art, often relating them to logical things.

Whole-brained people have a distinct advantage over people who favor their right brain or their left brain. If you want to become more whole-brained, there are several activities you can try. One of these is called the cross crawl. Because the left brain controls the right side of the body and the right brain controls the left side of the body, you are making your whole brain work together any time you make both sides work together at once. So stand up and lift your left knee, bringing your right hand down to touch it. Then touch your right knee with your left hand, and so on several times. As you keep doing this, you are getting the two sides of your brain to work together.

Another whole brained activity is to listen to words and music at the same time, provided they fit together and are felt as one experience. This sometimes happens in the movies, a television program or a radio show. One good example of this kind of activity is rap, in which the words and music go together, even if the music is only rhythm. So if you recite some of your lessons in the form of a rap, not only will that help you remember the material better, it will also help you become more whole-brained.

A third way of exercising your whole brain is to get the right side of your brain working by thinking about the overview of the subject you are studying, while using the left side of your brain to put the details in place. The more you move back and forth between overview and details, the more you are becoming whole brained in your thinking. An excellent way of doing this is to practice the mind mapping activity we introduced earlier.

THE TRIUNE (THREE PART) BRAIN

Another model of the brain is based on the idea of how it developed over millions of years. First there was the brain of the reptile or lizard. Dinosaurs were known for having very large bodies and comparatively tiny brains. That's because what their brains did was rather simple. They helped the dinosaur to survive by doing two basic kinds of things — attacking and running away.

THE DINOSAUR IN YOU

When the dinosaur was hungry, it went in search of prey. It attacked either plants or animals that it could eat. When it was in danger it tried to escape. It ran away. Perhaps Apatosaurus, with its huge legs could move just fast enough to get into the water up to its chin where the fearsome Tyrannosaurus Rex could not follow it.

Because dinosaurs were so large and so well adapted to their environment they could survive easily by looking around them to see their dinner or their danger. But the furry little mammals who dodged about their feet were not so lucky. They had to use other means to protect themselves and find their dinner.

THE WARM FUZZY IN YOU

These animals needed to hide in the woods and come out at night to hunt. That meant they couldn't depend on vision and had to develop their sense of smell and hearing. But vision is simple because you can easily tell where a thing is by looking at it. It's not so simple, though, to tell where it is from the sounds it makes or the smell it gives off. These senses require more complicated brain activity.

So the mammal's brain grew bigger and its methods of hunting and hiding more complex. These methods had to be learned, taught by the mammal parent and remembered by the young. This next part of the brain grown by the mammal contained the limbic system. This is the site of the complex emotions needed to raise a family and to learn complicated processes of tracking one's prey or hiding out to protect oneself. Here are the emotions that inspire both our pets and us to love and protect one another, to be excited by the sights and sounds and scents of a beautiful day, to fall in love, to nurture children, and to love to play. And here also is the access to the long term memory, for now that the mammals had to learn as they grew older, they had to remember what they learned.

Do elephants have bigger emotions?

THE COMPUTER SCIENTIST AND POET IN YOU

Why chimps don't do math

Human beings have grown a third part of their brains that the other animals do not have. This is called the neocortex, and it is the part that allows you to write poetry, do math problems, plan your day and enjoy music. It is the part that most specifically makes you human. The long term memory access is not found in the higher brain. So it is of little use to you unless it works well with the limbic system, for like other mammals we humans must learn as we grow older, love and protect each other, raise families, and build nests for ourselves. And we must remember much that we have learned for long periods of time.

HOW BEING AFRAID SHUTS DOWN YOUR BRAIN

Now the brain is so designed that whenever you're frightened you downshift into the part of your brain that powered the dinosaurs. You try to survive by attacking or fleeing. This works fine if you're standing in front of an oncoming train. You're not supposed to argue with the train or think about the philosophy or science of trains, you're just supposed to get out of the way, because if you don't you will die.

But it doesn't work so well in a classroom. Here you may suddenly become afraid that the teacher is going to call on you. But that doesn't mean you can hit the teacher, or run out of the room. Nor does it do any good to sit frozen in terror. Yet, as long as you're afraid, you can't think. You're as stupid as a dinosaur.

So if you're going to do well at learning something, you have to get over being afraid of it. If you're not able to learn, that probably means you've got some fear you can't get rid of.

ONE WAY TO GET RID OF FEAR

Getting rid of fear is easy when there is nothing really threatening you and you know how to do it. It is accomplished through practice.

While you are going to sleep at night, pick something you are a tiny bit afraid of. For example, you might pretend you're crossing the street and nearly get hit by a car, but easily jump out of the way. Or you might imagine you're going down hill in a roller coaster. Or that a bully that used to pick on you is doing so again. Or that you're about to be scolded by someone.

Imagine this thing you're afraid of is present in the room, coming at you, attacking you. See it clearly in your mind's eye. Then, again in your mind's eye, change it into something you like. Practice switching back and forth from the fearful thing to the thing that you like over and over again, until you've really got the hang of it.

Do this night after night until you're really good at it, using the thing that doesn't cause you too much anxiety.

After you're good at changing the slightly threatening thing into something you like, take something that's more threatening and repeat this process. When you've mastered that, go on to something even more threatening.

Eventually you'll be able to pick the things that you are most afraid of and change them in your mind into something you like. But you'll only be able to do this while you're going to sleep at night.

Now begin practicing during the day. Whenever something appears a little frightening but is not a real danger to you, mentally change the situation into one that you like. Practice this over and over until you get really good at it.

You should eventually get comfortable enough whenever you are threatened, to be able to think instead of freeze, and to do the wisest thing the situation calls for.

Any fears you may have of teachers or classrooms that could be keeping you from getting the most out of school will tend to disappear as you practice this technique.

THE STRONGER THE FEELING, THE BETTER THE MEMORY

When we study difficult material that doesn't interest us, we do not allow our limbic system and neocortex to work together. That's why it's often so hard to remember what we learn — because we have no strong feelings about it.

The things you do care about you find easy to remember. Maybe you collect baseball cards and can remember team players, scores, and games of long ago by the hundreds. Maybe you're a musician and can remember hundreds of songs. Maybe you're an expert on automobiles and can remember hundreds of facts about them. Whatever the case may be, you can easily see how much more fun it is to remember and learn something if you really care about it.

The moral is clear: If you want to learn something well, find something about it that excites you and makes you happy and interested in it. Every subject has the possibility of exciting you in this way, but only if you let it. You may have to use your imagination to find the fascination in some of your subjects, but if you do, you'll find them much easier to learn, and you'll also get higher grades in them.

BANISHING CLASSROOM BOREDOM

One method of turning something boring into something interesting is to relate it to your own interests. For example, if the teacher is talking about a period in history that has no meaning for you, look for things in the lecture that relate to someone or something you already know.

Suppose the teacher is talking about how the knights of the middle ages raised money so they could go on the crusades. You could then think about how you might apply that information to raise money for something you would like to do. If the teacher says they sold their land and you don't have any land to sell, think about what you do have that you could sell, such as your ideas or your time, and see if you can figure out a way to sell it. This habit of applying anything you hear to yourself can help you stay interested in the class material.

Here are some questions you can ask yourself to keep your mind on the subject matter:

How can I use this in my life?

How does this fit in with my own ideas — my philosophy of life?

How would the people I know react and feel in this story or historical event?

What would it feel like to be there? Sound like? Smell like? How would it look?

How is this related to the things I like to do?

Who am I going to explain this concept to or discuss this topic with?

How to get emotional about a subject.

Fill in some other questions

By doing these kinds of things you will be using more of your brain, avoiding fear and boredom, which keep you from thinking, and making your limbic system and your neocortex work together.

THE WHOLE PICTURE BRAIN

It used to be thought that memory is built up through a series of tiny bits of information, just as atoms get together to become molecules and molecules become cells and cells become organs and organs become bodies.

People believed that your memory for language worked this way too. Since language is made up of words, they thought the words must be learned first, then sentences, and so on. But this is not the case. Words are best learned as part of something larger: something that tells you about the words, something that makes up a story.

Just like details make more sense as part of the big picture

So it could be said that the basic unit of memory is the story. You can remember the parts of the story best because you remember the whole story. And each part of the story carries you into a different part of your brain. So each memory is spread all over the brain.

You can use this information about the brain to help you by making stories when you want to remember something. Suppose, for example, you want to remember a scientific concept like *photosynthesis* (the process by which plants convert light into food). Would you find this easier to learn and remember if it was defined as a formula using letters and symbols, or as a story about a Master Builder/Wizard (Chlorophyll: *Chlor — or phil?*) deep within the mysterious interior of a leaf who captures light energy from the sun to make the mighty fuel of his green empire: sugar. Taking a six pack of water ($6H_2O$), and a six pack of carbon dioxide ($6CO_2$), he busts them up into separate atoms, shuffles the pieces till he comes up with a precious molecule of sugar ($C_6H_{12}O_6$), and kicks the six leftover oxygen ($6O_2$) molecules out the window.

$$6H_2O + 6CO_2 = C_6H_{12}O_6 + 6O_2$$

or . . .

This is only one example of how you can constantly make up little stories (hopefully better than this one) to help you remember the connections you are trying to establish in your studying. Anything can be turned into a story, and it's easiest to remember if you make up your own.

THE BRAIN THAT GROWS LIKE THE FLOWERS IN SPRING

The fourth model we might call the self-growing brain. This suggests that the brain, just like a plant or a head of lettuce, can grow or wither depending on the kind of stimulation or thinking it is engaged in. In this view, the brain grows in richness and in quality when it is actively engaged in problem solving. But when it is not stimulated with opportunities to try something new, it withers like a dry leaf in the winter.

This model of the brain comes from many years of experimentation with rats. A researcher named Marian Diamond asked the following question: *Is it true that our brain stops growing after we are born and just decays, so that each time we lose some brain cells they are gone forever?*

She asked this question because at the time she began her research everyone believed that brain cells died throughout life and people got stupider as they got older, even though experience should have made them smarter.

HOW RAT BRAINS GROW

Diamond taught rats to do tricks. She then dissected their brains and compared them with those of rats which had not learned to do tricks. She found that the trained rats always had larger brains than the rats that were not trained.

This led to a startling conclusion about the brain: whenever you learn something your brain grows a little larger. The parts of the nerve cells that connect to other nerve cells (these are called dendrites) grow longer, so connections are made more easily. These cells grow as soon as you stimulate them.

So as people learn, they get smarter and their brains grow larger. Right now as you read this book and think about its relationship to your experience, new dendrites are growing in your brain and you are becoming a more effective, independent and smarter person.

INTELLIGENCE IS SOMETHING YOU LEARN

So it turns out there's no such thing as a fixed I.Q., an inherited intelligence that makes some people always smarter than others. Anyone, no matter how limited, can learn to be smarter. And anyone, no matter how smart, can eventually lose some intelligence, because when the brain is not exercised, the dendrites atrophy and the brain gets smaller.

The brain gets larger and smaller much the way our muscles do. Just as we strengthen our muscles, we can strengthen our brain — with thinking and problem-solving.

Thinking out loud and communicating our thoughts to others is especially important. The attention of a listener focuses our thinking — makes it matter more. Trying to help another person grasp and understand an idea forces us to develop it more thoroughly. How often do you give yourself a chance to think?

THINK-AND-LISTEN

Few of us are allowed to think in any responsible, independent way. When we do get around to telling others what's on our minds, we are usually interrupted. Other people butt in with advice, criticism, and other reactions almost instantly. Raw thinking is sensitive and easily sidetracked. Sometimes we never do get back to completing those ideas.

Think about what it would be like if you knew that from time to time you could be listened to while you said what you needed to say — without anyone butting in and telling you that what you were saying was all nonsense. This is such an important and rewarding experience we've developed a little exercise about it that we call a **Think-and-Listen**.

When we do a **Think-and-Listen**, we make a deal to listen to another person for five minutes or more without any interruption whatever. We look the person straight in the eye and express without words that we support what is being said. But we do not interrupt. In exchange, we get a turn to be listened to as well.

It's as simple as that. Two people agree to listen to each other for a certain period of time without interrupting, and they then take turns talking and listening.

You can do Think-and-Listens to solve problems, or to come up with creative new ideas, or to really nail down and explore a topic in school. Think-and-Listens are great for sorting out problems in a relationship too.

THE RULES FOR A THINK-AND-LISTEN:

1. Find a partner.
2. Agree in advance on the amount of time to be used by each person, and keep track of it.
3. Decide which of you will talk first, and which will listen first.
4. Establish confidentiality of whatever is said, and agree that it will never be discussed later unless the person who said it suggests doing so.
5. Trade roles when your talking time is up.
6. The listener must maintain eye contact with the talker.
7. The talker must not attack the listener.
8. The listener may not interrupt to make comments or ask questions of the talker at any time.
9. Allow for feedback after each one has had equal time to talk, if both desire this.
10. If you are the talker, use the exact agreed upon time and don't trade away what is rightfully yours, even if you believe you have said everything you wanted to say.

YOUR SEVEN INTELLIGENCES

Your brain wants to do much more than you're likely to be asked to do in school. It has at least seven different types of intelligence, of which school usually asks you to use only two — math/logic and language. In other words, in school you are expected to reason about things, give correct answers to logical questions and do math. You are also expected to understand, read, write, and speak your native language well. These are all important skills.

But you also have five other kinds of intelligence that are just as important as math/logic and language, and school doesn't ask you to make much use of them. If it did, you'd probably have a much easier time and would learn a lot more.

Let's look at your other intelligences and think about how they might be used in your schoolwork. Some will mean more to you than others, because each of us develops a preference for different intelligences.

We'll also suggest some exercises that stimulate each intelligence and these may help you do better in school. Some exercises may appeal to you more than others, because some of your intelligences may be stronger than others. So you might start out by using the exercises that work best for you now. As you experiment with less comfortable exercises, though, you may find that your less-developed intelligences are getting stronger, too.

YOUR SPATIAL INTELLIGENCE

In addition to the first two intelligences we've mentioned (logic and language), you have a third intelligence called visual, or spatial. This part of your brain likes to think in pictures and spatial relationships. Graphs, pictures, charts, maps, diagrams and other visual aids stimulate this capacity of your brain. Try the following three exercises, or tricks, and see if they help your studying.

Draw pictures

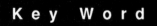

Trick # 1: You can take notes in pictures. Did you know that for every word you consciously think, you have an equivalent picture in your mind?

If you take notes in pictures, you'll find that it's much easier to remember the ideas you're studying, because it's easier to remember pictures than words. Decide which words of your text (or your notes or a lecture) are the most important and express each word with a picture. Let's call these words **key words**, because they are the key to unlocking the information that surrounds them.

For example, in the sentence *"You can take notes in pictures,"* the key words might be **notes** and **pictures**. In the sentence *"Did you know that for every word you consciously think, you have an equivalent picture in your mind,"* the key words might be **word** and **equivalent picture**. Note that in this last example, the key word consists of two words, both needed to capture the complete key word meaning.

Hint: Until you've practiced this exercise quite a bit, you might forget what the pictures mean. So start by writing the key words and the pictures in your notes. Then memorize the pictures (which you'll probably find quite easy) and see if they bring back the key words. If they don't, do more work on your pictures so they express the words better or are more detailed. That way, both the words and pictures will be easier to remember.

Trick # 2: You can take notes in the form of **Mind Maps** like the ones we discussed in Chapter 7.

Mind Mapping

Taking notes in maps lets you group ideas as you go. It also gives you a structure in which to store your key word pictures and their relationships. As you get good at this, you'll be able to remember large amounts of information easily.

Hint: Ideas relate to each other in many different ways. Work with your Mind Maps so the relationships they show are useful ones. Check them out through class discussion, and keep experimenting with new ways of finding relationships between ideas. Don't be upset if some of your relationships don't make sense to other people. It's fun to explain to others how you see things — and keep an open mind, yourself, to different points of view.

Trick # 3: If you want to remember to do something, **imagine a connection** between that activity and something else. For example, if you want to remember to feed your pet frog as soon as you get home from school, imagine the frog sitting on your doorknob. Then when you arrive home and look at the doorknob, it will remind you to feed the frog.

Visualize associations

Hint: Don't blame the process if it doesn't work at first. With practice you'll improve your ability to remember things you have to do. Whenever it fails, improve your visualization so it will stick in your memory better the next time you use it.

YOUR KINESTHETIC INTELLIGENCE

The fourth intelligence we'll consider is called kinesthetic. The word *kinesthetic* (pronounced *kin-iss-thetic*) refers to the body's sense of its own movement through space. You are using your kinesthetic intelligence when you think with your body. Recent brain research suggests the most effective way to process new ideas is to relate them to experiences involving the body.

Whenever you move, your kinesthetic intelligence is operating. In order to be good at dance or sports, you have to develop this intelligence well. By learning how to relate your body to ideas you encounter in school, you can lay a stronger foundation for understanding the ideas than you can any other way. In fact, the word "understanding" suggests this. Your legs stand under your body, creating a foundation for your entire stance.

Here are some exercises using your kinesthetic intelligence.

Trick # 4: When you read a description of an activity, **imagine doing it yourself**. That's easy if you're reading a novel with lots of action, but you can also do it with textbooks.

Act it out in your imagination

For example, suppose you're reading a passage about the structure of the atom, which says that electrons move around a nucleus made of protons and neutrons. It will be easier to remember this if you imagine you are physically part of the atom. Close your eyes and pretend you're standing on a proton. Look at the other protons next to you. Then look at the neutrons. Imagine the electrons moving all around you as if they were planets in their orbits.

When you read textbooks in this imaginative way, it will be easy to learn a great deal of information, because you can keep adding it to the drama you're creating. This exercise works best if you imagine you're actually moving among the various images you've created, feeling the relationship of your own body to what you're pretending to see around you.

Hint: The first time you do this, don't go too fast. Read a sentence or two, then close your eyes, breathe deeply, and daydream about what you've just read. Take enough time to make the daydream detailed and lively.

Feel it in your body

Trick # 5: Sometimes abstract ideas are easier to understand if you think about how they might be expressed in **dance**. In the privacy of your own room, consider an abstract idea like "addition" or "freedom" or "osmosis," and try moving your body so it expresses the idea. You may or may not be satisfied with your expression, but just trying to dance the idea will help you understand it better.

Hint: Don't get self-conscious about this — no one's looking! If you can't imagine being a dancer, perhaps you can turn the idea into a game and play with it that way. Pretend a chemical reaction is a football play. How would it be arranged on the field? If you were one of the players, how would you move?

YOUR MUSICAL INTELLIGENCE

The fifth intelligence stored in your brain is the musical intelligence. This is the part of you that likes to sing, play an instrument, listen to music, or perhaps even make up music of your own. You can use music in many ways to help you do better in school. Here are a few examples.

Sing it

Trick # 6: If you have to memorize a set of facts — like math formulas or historical dates — it's easier if you make them into a **song or rap**. (Remember learning your ABCs with the alphabet song?) Make up your own verses about the material you have to learn, and sing them to one of your favorite tunes or chants.

Hint: You might think you've memorized a song before you actually have. Sing the song a few times, and then go back to it the next day. After several days of reviewing the song, you should be able to remember the material for many years.

Use your subconscious

Trick # 7: James was having trouble in his math classes because he had never learned his multiplication tables. He recorded the tables he didn't know on a cassette tape and listened to his recording. Because the tape was boring all by itself, though, he needed something else to make it enjoyable. He found that if he played his favorite **music** loudly while the tape was playing softly, his subconscious mind would memorize the multiplication tables while his conscious mind was listening to the music.

This technique works best, James found, with Baroque, Classical, or Romantic music. That's because those three types of music seem to make the brain more receptive to remembering things. The trick here is not to worry about hearing the multiplication table (or whatever you're trying to remember). By listening to the *music*, and allowing yourself to enjoy that experience, you are decreasing your resistance to hearing and remembering the multiplication table.

In a week, James had learned his multiplication tables so well that math became much easier for him, and he grew to love his math courses. You can do what James did — not just with the multiplication tables, but with any relatively simple collection of facts you'd like to remember the rest of your life.

YOUR INTELLIGENCE THAT GETS ALONG WITH OTHER PEOPLE

The sixth intelligence is called the inter-personal intelligence and it helps you get along with others. If you have lots of friends and enjoy parties, and if people turn to you for leadership and advice, you may have a strong inter-personal intelligence. Here's how you can use it to improve your schoolwork.

Trick # 8: Some people think it's cheating to **study together** in groups. But forming a study group may be one of the most important things you can do to help yourself. In Chapter 11 you'll find lots of tips for setting up a study group and getting the most out of it. Use the group to decide how much time to spend on each study task. Join together to figure out how to make the material you are studying more interesting and easier to understand.

Do it with your friends

Hint: Remember that study groups work best when everyone in the group has an equally important role. Don't be a parasite, and don't let your study partners be parasites, either. Everyone should make an equal contribution.

Trick # 9: When you and your study partners have to cover a great deal of material, **divide up** the reading **assignments** equally. Each member of the group can then report to the others on the individual sections. That way, each person will have read part of the material thoroughly, and everyone will have discussed all the material.

Many hands make light work

Hint: With this technique, it is extremely important that each person who is reporting really understand the material studied. If you have an assignment to report on to the group and you don't understand it, find someone who can explain it to you before it is time for you to make your report. Otherwise, the group may miss getting some important information. So allow yourself plenty of time. That way, if there's something in the material you don't understand, there will be enough time so the rest of the group will not miss the material you are responsible for.

YOUR INTELLIGENCE OF SELF-KNOWLEDGE

The seventh intelligence helps you understand yourself. It's called the intra-personal intelligence. Understanding yourself in new ways helps you understand new ideas.

Here are two ways to explore the subjects you're studying by relating them to your personal interests, values, and concerns.

Trick # 10: Pick a passage in your textbook that contains important information you want to remember. Make sure you understand the ideas, and then **relate each idea to something in your own experience**. Let's use

Make it relevant

the atom example. You might say an atom is like a family. The protons and neutrons are like a married couple, while the electrons resemble children. That's why the electrons can fly off and join other atoms, which the protons and neutrons normally don't do. By making this comparison, you can relate the atom to something basic in your own life. We call this, making an analogy.

Hint: You can easily make false analogies with this technique. There are many things about atoms that are not at all like families, so that comparison might tempt you to read things into the atomic structure that are not accurate. Use only the parts of your analogy that correctly reflect the idea you're learning.

TAKE SOME TIME TO RELAX AND ENJOY THE SCENERY

Trick # 11: ***Put on some music that makes you feel calm and peaceful*** (even if it sounds like elevator music). Close your eyes and let the images of the material you're studying come into your mind. Gently play with the images, let them dance to the music, and get to know them. This will give you a new, more personal feeling about the ideas you're studying.

Relax

Hint: Don't force this technique. Give the music time to do its work. The most important part is getting completely relaxed, so the images come to mind easily and gently. Don't give up if you've listened to the music for five or ten minutes and nothing's come to mind. If you are patient, the images will eventually come to you.

YOU ARE HOW YOU USE YOUR BRAIN

When you think about the question '*who am I?*' relate it to the way your brain works and what you're doing about that. Use the different models we've described above to look at how you think and why you think the way you do.

You may very well find strengths and talents in yourself that you had not recognized, or didn't know how to develop until now. At the same time, clear away some of the obstacles to learning that may be interfering with your full use of your wonderful brain. Expand your thinking processes, tap into that potential, and you will create opportunities to become many things you may have only dreamed about until now.

T r y   T h i s ☞   Imagine that your car has broken down in the desert. Which intelligence will be most helpful to you? Discuss this problem with one or a group of friends.

10

Your Learning Style: One Key To Your Success

In this chapter we'll take a look at how the different ways people like to learn can affect their success at what they do. We're all different, but we can all learn, each in our own special way. This chapter will be exciting for you, because it will give you an opportunity to figure out your own learning style as you read. This may change how you do many of the things you've been doing. It may be that as you study you ought to have something to munch in your hand, or some music playing. But because you've been told not to do those things while studying, you haven't been doing it, even though it would be the right thing for you. So read on and see how many of the different categories of learning style apply to you. By the time you're finished reading this, you'll know yourself a lot better.

THE MISERABLE EDUCATION OF POOR TYRONE

Once upon a time there was a boy named Tyrone. Tyrone was a complete failure in school. Nothing he did ever worked. When the teacher told the students to sit down, he wanted to be up out of his chair, moving around. When the teacher said no food was allowed in the classroom, Tyrone found he was terribly hungry. When the teacher said it was time to read, Tyrone found the light too bright, and the silence in the room deafening. Tyrone liked to learn things by touching them, not by reading about them. He liked to talk over what he learned with others. And he found the best time for him to learn was from twelve noon until four o'clock in the afternoon.

By the time he was in eighth grade, Tyrone was a recognized disaster area. His parents had been called in many times, but this particular time in a somber meeting with the principal, six school counselors and a few outside experts, Tyrone was expecting the worst.

SAVED BY . . . LEARNING STYLES?!

Things turned out differently, however. The outside expert was an authority on learning styles. Tyrone had been given a learning styles assessment and the expert had returned to give the report and recommendations. As it happened, Tyrone soon realized this stranger was the best friend he had ever had in his life.

"It seems that Tyrone is not able to learn in school," said the expert patiently, "because nothing that happens in school appeals to his particular set of learning styles. None of the classrooms he has ever been in has been organized to accommodate him. If he were allowed to study under the conditions that favor his study preferences, it would soon be seen that he is in fact capable of highly original thinking."

The expert's advice was listened to and taken. A whole new set of study conditions were set up for Tyrone. Soon he was at the very top of his class. When it was time for graduation from high school, Tyrone was the valedictorian. He acquired a Ph.D. in Chemisty and published seven learned and scholarly books before he reached the age of thirty, and lived happily ever after.

But had the outside expert not taken his side, Tyrone might very well have spent the rest of his life feeling like a failure.

DESPITE YOUR GROUP IDENTITY, YOU'RE STILL UNIQUE

Each of us is a unique individual who has something to contribute to the world that no one else can possibly contribute. Your mission is to discover that special gift to the world that makes you different from everyone else. This special quality of yours is in some ways the most important thing about you. You should learn to treasure it.

THE MISTAKE EDUCATORS HAVE MADE

Until recently most educators thought everyone should be taught at the same pace, and with the same teaching and study methods — that all of us learn in approximately the same ways. "Listen carefully, pay attention to what I am saying, study hard and you'll learn," teachers would command. "If you do not master the material, it's your own fault."

Now we know better. People learn in many different ways. Conditions which can help one person learn can actually interfere with learning for another.

YOU AND YOUR LEARNING STYLE

Each person, including you, has a unique learning style, just as we all have unique finger prints.

Your unique style of learning is one of the most important things about you. It is among your greatest advantages in life.

No one else learns quite the way you do. You probably differ markedly from your best friend in how you pay attention and think about things. Most likely your teacher and your mother don't learn in the same ways you do either. As a result of these natural differences, your parents or teachers may ask you to use study methods that are not necessarily the best ones for you. A mother who learns most things through her ears may have trouble understanding why her son doesn't ever seem to have heard what she has told him. He may not be able to understand a new idea well until he sees it or acts it out with his body. Thus differences in learning can cause

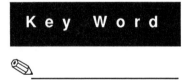

misunderstandings between teachers, parents and students.

Is it possible that some of whatever trouble you may have had in school is because your learning style does not fit what the school expects of you? Wouldn't you be happier if school expected you to be what you are?

ENJOY YOUR DIFFERENCES, YOU CAN'T ESCAPE THEM

Our differences make us able to contribute something that no one else can offer. They give us the qualities that others are most likely to admire. So rejoice in the fact that you're unique in your style of learning, and make the best use of it.

The way you learn is not like a style of dressing or behaving that you can simply copy from other students or teachers. In many ways, it will remain uniquely and stubbornly your own, no matter what you do. Fortunately, you can make this uniqueness work to your advantage.

By knowing what works best for you, you can use your abilities to the fullest, and can create many learning opportunities for yourself. The important thing is to recognize, understand and use your own learning style. Fortunately, this is not a difficult thing to do. In fact, most people find it fascinating and exciting to discover their own strengths and the ways to use them.

IDENTIFYING YOUR LEARNING STYLE

There are several different approaches to analyzing and identifying the varying learning styles of individuals. Perhaps the most comprehensive and widely used system of all was developed by Drs. Rita and Kenneth Dunn. It examines about twenty characteristics which apply to everyone, regardless of age.

Every person has about six to twelve characteristics which directly influence his or her success in learning. Many of us are drastically influenced by several of these elements, and our ability to concentrate, focus attention and learn successfully will have a lot to do with whether these conditions are present or absent.

Here's how learning styles are determined in the system developed by the Dunns: A hundred item questionnaire which determines preferences on about twenty elements of learning style is given to the student. It takes about 30 to 40 minutes to complete. Then it can be scored and interpreted. (Ask your teacher, guidance counselor or school principal for a *Dunn, Dunn and Price Learning Styles Inventory* assessment. Backed by extensive research, it is widely used in schools.) There is also a version for home use called **Amazing Grades** by Dr. Kenneth Dunn which includes a testing questionnaire and lots of ideas to help you set up your ideal learning conditions.

22 IMPORTANT KINDS OF DIFFERENCES

The following is an introduction to the elements of learning styles identified by the Dunns. They can be grouped into five categories: environmental, emotional, learning groups, sensory and biological.

Which factors are important for you?

As you read through these 22 items, see whether you feel a strong reaction like, "gosh, that's me". Then the next time you study, especially some new or difficult subject, experiment with those elements that you feel strongly about. For example, if you read or study better under dim light, then request it at home or school, and see if your studying becomes more productive. If other people try to block you or wonder why you are doing this, refer them to the information in this chapter.

A GUIDE TO THE ELEMENTS OF LEARNING STYLES

ENVIRONMENT

1. **Noise level** — quiet or sound. Some people need quiet when they are learning, while others notice neither noise nor movement once they begin to concentrate; they can block out sound. Some people need sound. They turn on a radio, or stereo and listen to some instrumental music whenever they study, as a screen against random noise distractions. Others are not comfortable unless there is noise and activity around them as they work.

2. **Light** — low or bright. Some people work best under very bright light. Others find bright light harsh and irritating. They need dim or low light in order to concentrate.

3. **Temperature** — cool or warm. Many students can't think when they feel hot, and others can't when they feel cold.

4. **Setting** — informal or formal. Many students think best in a formal environment — seated on wooden, steel, or plastic chairs like those found in conventional classrooms, a library, or a kitchen. However some learn better in an informal environment — on a lounge chair, a bed, the floor, on pillows, or on carpeting.

EMOTIONS AND ATTITUDES

5. **Motivation**. Motivation is the desire to achieve academically. Some people are positive about going to school and get involved in their studies. Others are not so interested in their studies or other school activities.

6. **Persistence**. This element involves your inclination either to complete tasks that are begun or to take intermittent breaks and return to assignments or learning activities later.

7. **Responsibility**. This element involves your desire to do what you think you ought to. In schools, responsibility often is related to conformity or following through on what a teacher asks you to do. Some people have no trouble folowing directions and meeting the teachers demands. Others may feel irritated and turned off when they are asked to complete a task a certain way. They prefer to have more of a say in how a responsibility is carried out.

8. Needs or does not need **structure**. This element involves your need for specific directions or explanation prior to undertaking or completing an assignment. Some people want to be told exactly how to proceed. Others prefer to complete an assignment in their own way.

LEARNING GROUPS

9. **Learning alone**. Some individuals prefer to study by themselves.

10. **Pairs**. Some prefer to learn with one other person.

11. **Teams**. Some prefer working in a group where discussion and interaction facilitate learning.

12. **Authority figure present**. You might feel more comfortable when a person with authority or recognized special knowledge is present, perhaps a teacher or parent.

13. **Prefers Variety**. This element may have two different meanings. It suggests that the person may learn easily alone, and also with other people present (peers, or with an authority or in any combination); or that the person needs variety, as opposed to routine.

SENSORY

14. **Auditory** preferences. This perceptual area describes people who can learn best by listening to a verbal instruction such as a lecture, discussion or recording.

15. Preference for **Seeing Words**. Maybe you are a learner who learns primarily by seeing and reading words.

16. **Seeing Pictures**. Maybe you are a learner whose primary perceptual strength is visual and therefore can recall what you have seen or observed; such people, when asked for information from printed or diagrammatic material, can close their eyes and recall what they have seen earlier.

17. **Touching**. If your perceptual strengths are tactile, then you need to touch things in order to learn well. You can learn best by examining models and other three dimensional objects. Underline as you read, take notes when you listen and keep your hands busy — particularly if you also have low auditory ability.

18. **Doing/moving**. If you're a learner with kinesthetic preferences, you require whole body movement and/or real life experiences if you are to absorb and retain material to be learned. Such people learn most easily when they are totally involved. Acting, puppetry, and drama are examples of kinesthetic learning; others include building, designing, visiting, interviewing and playing.

BIOLOGICAL

19. **Requires intake**. This element describes those students who often eat, drink, chew or bite objects while concentrating — as opposed to those who prefer no intake until after they have finished studying.

20. **Time of day**. People differ in their daily rhythms of alertness. When is your best time of day for maximum concentration: early morning, late morning, afternoon, or evening? Learn new material and difficult subjects at your best time of day.

21. **Mobility**. How quietly can you sit — and for how long? Some people need frequent breaks and must move about the environment. Others can sit for hours while engaged in learning — particularly if the task interests them.

22. **Global/Analytic**. Global learners like to see the whole picture first. Analytic learners like to start at the beginning and proceed step by step.

Few students are influenced by all of these learning styles elements, but most are positively affected by at least 6 to 12 of them. And they may shift over time. Learning environments you prefer in 7th, 8th or 9th grade might be altogether different from those you might choose when you are out of high school.

YOU MIGHT APPLY THIS INFORMATION RIGHT NOW

Perhaps you already have an idea of how important some of these elements are to you. If you do, then you can experiment with changing your study situation so you are getting more of what you need.

One common example of changes that can easily be made to satisfy a clear preference has to do with the very first element. Some people like to study with music around them — often a radio playing instrumental (not vocal) music — while others prefer quiet. If you know which you prefer, then make sure that is what you get. Parents and teachers often discourage people from studying while they have the radio playing. If you're having that problem, show a parent or teacher this chapter, suggest that you might do better if you're allowed to study with music playing and suggest that you be allowed to do an experiment: can you bring up your grades if you are allowed to study to music?

Perhaps thinking about your preferences will lead you to recognize that you might learn better if you're in an environment where you can get up and walk around while you think about the material you're studying. Or you might want to have food and drink handy when you study. Or perhaps you'll do better studying at certain times of the day than at others.

So go back over all the categories listed above, think about how each may or may not affect you, and then come up with a list of proposed changes in the way you study and the conditions under which you study. This could make a big difference in your success as a student.

My Learning Style Preferences   **Things I Can Do To Help Myself**

_____   _____

_____   _____

_____   _____

_____   _____

_____   _____

_____   _____

My Learning Style Preferences	Things I Can Do To Help Myself
_____	_____
_____	_____
_____	_____
_____	_____
_____	_____
_____	_____

YOU'LL DO BETTER ONCE YOU KNOW YOUR PREFERENCES

Knowing your preferences can make a significant difference in your academic achievement. If the teacher knows the learning style of all the students, then the class experience can be designed to take into account all the differences among the students. How material is presented, how tests are given, how studying takes place and how the class is involved in group interaction can all make a contribution to greater achievement and success.

Suppose, for example, you happen to prefer dim light and a warm environment with an opportunity to move around a lot. Most schools are bright, and not so warm, and require you to sit in your chair, not allowing you to get up and move around in order to better integrate your learning. This would probably make things a lot more difficult for you, possibly causing frustration, anxiety and boredom.

Dozens of research reports show that most students do much better when they are taught under circumstances that take their learning styles into account.

Even if your teachers are unaware of learning styles at this time, you can improve your chances of success in school by knowing your preferences and acting accordingly whenever you are trying to learn something. Wear a sweater if you're cold, sit by the window if you need lots of light.

Also, you have enough information right here to ask your teacher, counselor or principal to investigate the use of the *Dunn, Dunn and Price Learning Styles Inventory (LSI)* for you and your classmates.

BEING DIFFERENT CAN CAUSE CONFUSION ON THE HOME FRONT

By the way, it might interest you to know that parents tend to be opposite from each other in their learning styles. Also, brothers and sisters are likely to differ greatly in theirs. That means that the average family of four may have arguments and disagreements because they perceive and process information differently. If you take this into account in thinking about your family, it may help to make life happier and more manageable for you.

Expect to be different even from other family members

Here are ways that the people in my family learn differently

_____

_____

_____

_____

_____

Respect other people's learning styles —and your own

ENJOY THE TREASURES THAT MAKE YOU WHAT YOU ARE

In conclusion, think of your differences as your personal treasures — like your voice print or toe print — unique to you and valuable to your strengths and capacities. As you can see, there are many learning styles and lots of different ways of perceiving the world and processing the data you take in with your eyes, ears, nose and other senses. Recognizing this can help you create learning opportunities for yourself, instead of just accepting and coping with the traditional learning situations.

You can improve your learning opportunities by respecting your individuality, while pursuing quality in the many different ways in which you function best.

Celebrate the differences in others and the diversity around you. Discover your strong learning capacities (you have many, many of them) and happily build them into a complete set of tools for getting the most out of life.

Try This ☞ Get together with a friend and compare your different learning styles.

11

Turning Defeat Into Victory

In this chapter you'll have a chance to see how you can turn the failures in your life into successes. In fact a failure turned into a success often makes a better kind of success than one without a failure behind it. One major way of doing this is asking for help, a skill many of us have been taught to believe is cheating, or a sign of weakness. It's not. Asking for help and being part of a support group are both ways to become strong, and we'll learn about them here. The result could be to help you put more A's on your report card, add a great deal of fun to studying, and build a better, more rewarding social life.

LEARNING FROM FAILURES IN SCHOOL

Failing a test or falling behind in a course can challenge your feelings of competence as a student. The problem of failure arises for all students at some time — and for some students all the time.

You might not believe it, but failure is not necessarily bad. By challenging us with difficult situations, school gives us an opportunity to practice problem-solving. As a result, we become better equipped to solve problems we'll have later in life. But this happens only if we become skilled at studying our failures and losses so we can learn from them.

> **Failure Is An Opportunity To Practice Problem-Solving**

DON'T GIVE UP ON YOURSELF

Humboldt had never been taught to deal with failure. Whenever he fell behind, he found himself abandoned to a pattern of increasing failure. Soon he was classified as a problem and sometimes even regarded as a hopeless case. He was criticized by some who thought they were superior because they were able to succeed where he had failed.

Imagine what would happen if doctors treated sick people the way teachers, parents and fellow students treated Humboldt. Did you ever hear a doctor say "He's got a cold — punish him! Take away his medicine!" Failure in school is not a terminal illness, or a crime. It's not even necessarily a "problem." Viewed properly, it's an opportunity for learning, correction, and improvement.

Because there are so many negative social attitudes toward failure, all of us, like Humboldt, are likely to be too critical of ourselves when we fail. We may decide we are lazy, stupid, no good, and other things that are really not true of us. As a result, the problem of failure is aggravated and may begin to seem hopeless. That's probably why so many students drop-out from so many educational programs.

If loss of hope as a result of failure can occur in school, it can also occur in life. Therefore, we must learn to recognize when we are falling behind, so we can do something about it.

THE IMPORTANCE OF ASKING FOR HELP

What can you do once you become aware that you're stuck and falling behind? Andrea discovered that the first step was to ask for help. She found that if she discovered the trouble quickly and sought help right away, it was never difficult to catch up and ultimately succeed. Asking for help might be hard for you, though. This difficulty may occur for one of two reasons.

IT'S NOT CHEATING TO ASK FOR HELP

To begin with, asking for help might seem like cheating. Irving would often think to himself: "I ought to be able to solve this problem by myself; therefore, if I get someone to help me, that's cheating." He never asked for help and found himself forever behind. Ultimately, Irving dropped out of school. His problems continued to get worse and worse, but he still believed it would be cheating to get anyone to help him.

Some kinds of help are, indeed, cheating. But in the long run, cheating cheats the cheater more than anyone else, because the cheater doesn't get a chance to learn from the experience. So if someone gets you through a difficult situation without giving you any idea how to handle it on your own, that may be cheating. For example, if you try to get someone to tell you the answers to a test — that's cheating. Or if you borrow money you don't intend ever to pay back — that's cheating.

But the right kind of help can get you back on the track after you've fallen behind in your studies (or in life). Asking for the kind of help that shows you how to answer your questions and solve your problems is one of the keys to success. And it's never cheating.

ISN'T ASKING FOR HELP A SIGN OF WEAKNESS?

When we consider asking for help, though, we may fall into a second kind of trap. Philip often reasoned this way: "The fact that I cannot do this by myself means I am inadequate. I ought to be able to figure it out on my own, and I will stick to it until I do." Then he would fail and give up, ignoring or denying that he had a problem.

Like Philip we're all inadequate at times, but our inadequacies don't need to defeat us. The trouble is that just like Philip, when we feel we are doing poorly, we are all too likely to compare ourselves not with any one person, but collectively with everyone in the group who is doing well. We do not allow for the fact that each successful person has some inadequacies, many of which may not be visible to others. So perhaps we say, "I am the worst person here."

Meanwhile, other members of the group may be feeling that way about themselves too.

Sometimes we carry the rejection of help to extremes. Angela was the kind of person who would say, whenever help was offered to her, "I don't need this — I'm fine as I am." She would then go on to try something at which she could not possibly succeed, only to fail — often for a second, third, or fourth time. How much easier it would have been for her to accept the offered help instead of toughing it out and achieving nothing.

IT TAKES PERSONAL STRENGTH TO ASK FOR HELP

The mistaken impression Angela had that refusing help is a sign of strength only caused her trouble and ended by making her much weaker than she otherwise would have been. There's nothing weak about asking for help, but there may be a great deal of weakness in not asking for it. Let's think a little about why this is.

If you're always trying to prove how strong you are, that shows you really don't think you are strong, or you wouldn't have to put so much energy into trying to prove it.

By refusing help when she needed it, Angela was saying, "I don't believe I'm strong, but I have to prove that I am, so I'm going to refuse your help."

As a result she missed many opportunities to become stronger. She continued feeling weak, and thus continued having to try to prove she was strong by refusing more help.

Meanwhile, the truly strong, who are not afraid to ask for help, get stronger. Thus, even though we may think it's a badge of honor to succeed on our own, the opposite is actually the case. Those who know how to get and use help deserve the highest honors.

So next time there's a possibility you might need help, prove how strong you are by asking for it! And if someone asks you for help, do your best to give them the help they need.

Here are my attitudes about failure

_____

_____

_____

BUILD A GOOD RELATIONSHIP WITH YOUR TEACHER

Once you decide you need help, the solution may be to go to your teacher to get it. This will be easier if you have established a good relationship with the teacher to begin with. Most teachers form their impressions of their students quite early in the year, so it's wise to make a good impression from the beginning.

If your teachers think you're not interested, or not trying, they may not want to bother helping you. But if you've shown you really care about the work and want to succeed at it, teachers are more likely to want to devote extra time to help you.

One thing you might do at the beginning of each course is have a talk with the teacher, in which you ask for guidance about what kinds of study will work best in the class. From time to time, show your teacher the questions you've written in your notebooks and workbooks. Ask for feedback. Most teachers appreciate and value the student who is eager to find out how to do well. So, if you can, cultivate a positive relationship — perhaps even a friendship — with your teacher.

RELATING WELL TO YOUR TEACHERS

Perhaps you've never given much thought to the idea that teachers are people too. And even though not all teachers are helpful all the time, most people go into teaching because they want to be helpful. Sometimes it's not their fault if they don't know what would be the most helpful to their students.

If you're having trouble understanding your teacher, building a relationship may help a great deal to break down the barriers between you. Besides, you'll learn a lot about how to deal effectively with other people who may play an important role in your life.

THE IMPORTANCE OF KEEPING YOUR WORD

You can't get respect if you don't keep your word

Of course you can't have real communication if you don't mean what you say. We all want others to like us, and that is good. But sometimes because of our desire to please others we make promises we can't really keep. We do this to get their approval at the time, but it backfires on us later when the promise is broken. It's a great way to lose the trust and respect of others, and if you do it a lot, you'll end up with really bad relationships.

So think about the importance of whatever you say. People will tend to believe you if you keep your word all the time. After you have broken it a few times, it will get around that you are a liar and not to be trusted. Then you'll have trouble getting anyone to believe you about anything. This may not seem to matter much at first, but it will cost you a great deal in the long run, because many of the opportunities you might otherwise have had for friendship and good relationships will be gone — if not forever, for a long time to come.

REPLACE EXCUSE-MAKING WITH FRIENDSHIP

Where do you start? You can begin with a simple rule that will probably look easier to say than to follow, at least until you've put it into practice: Don't make excuses to your teachers, even if the excuses are valid.

It might seem reasonable to explain to the teacher why you were late if you unexpectedly got caught in a traffic jam. But the reason won't affect the results. If you are not in class, you are not in a position to know what happened while you were missing.

You'll find that if you stop giving others excuses you'll stop looking for them, and as a result you will need fewer of them. Then you'll meet your obligations more often and more successfully.

Instead of making excuses, take the trouble to get to know your teacher. Some teachers really like spending time with their students and giving them extra help. If you can, make an appointment to see your teacher and discuss the class, your work, and any confusions you may have. Most teachers are eager to help you understand the material better, or at least figure out what to do to make it easier to understand. Some teachers will go to a great deal of trouble to try to help you because they really care whether you learn or not.

GIVING YOUR TEACHER GOOD ATTENTION

In return for the attention you get from the teacher, you should give good attention back. Be attentive in class. Respond well to the teacher's requests. Always do what is asked if you can, but if for some reason you can't, explain why without making excuses.

Be prepared, also, to accept and respond to the teacher's criticism. It is usually given in the spirit of trying to help you do better. Good criticism, remember, is a gift, and you can do a lot with it. It may not feel good to get the criticism when it is given to you, but once you have corrected the problem, you will not get that kind of criticism anymore. You will be a better person, you will be doing better work, and you will have had a chance to see just how much good the criticism did you.

Remember — good feedback helps you to reach *your* goals

As for your behavior in class, arrive early, do good work, and participate fully in the class. The teacher will find your presence there pleasing and rewarding.

Go out of your way as often as possible to tell the teacher what you like about the class. This kind of appreciation is something most teachers get too little of. They do the best they can, and, like everyone else, they would like to know when they've done their job well. You can make quite a difference in a teacher's whole day by going up after class and saying what you liked about it. Then, if you have a complaint once in a while, the teacher is more likely to listen and react positively to it.

BE ASSERTIVE, BUT NOT AGGRESSIVE

Finally, in your communication with teachers and other people, it's a good idea to be assertive without being aggressive. That means you should stand up for what you believe is important, but not go around picking fights with people, which will only get you in trouble. No one wants to deal with a person who is always apologizing or being shy. Approach the other person in a friendly, confident way, showing that you like yourself and also the person you are talking to. Don't attempt to overpower the other person or make him or her feel self-conscious. Just be warm and friendly, and express yourself strongly.

School can give you the opportunity to practice and master communication skills which will always be useful to you. And one of the most valuable things you can learn is how to get more out of your relationships with others.

_____

_____

_____

Competition doesn't always bring out our best

COOPERATIVE GROUPS MAKE PEOPLE FEEL UP TO THE JOB

In groups that work cooperatively, the problems of inadequacy and the feeling of failure usually don't arise. When people are working together towards a common goal, each person has an interest in the success of others. Individuals compensate for each other's inadequacies, which helps to overcome them, while the group as a whole grows strong.

When people are competing, though, differences in knowledge or ability tend to get interpreted as differences in degrees of personal inadequacy. Often, even when you are doing something well, you may feel as if you are no good because you are not doing it well enough. (Sometimes, by contrast, you might want to do poorly so you won't make others look bad.)

When you're not performing well, the likely reason is that you don't want to bother, or that the thing you are attempting is too hard for you at the moment. With more instruction and practice, you will eventually be able to do it well.

CREATE YOUR OWN STUDY GROUP

So why not set up a support system or study group from which all members can benefit by exchanging help? This is a wonderful way to improve everyone's schoolwork, because it also brings the members closer together, helping to build positive, worthwhile friendships. In addition, it teaches valuable skills of cooperation useful in many situations outside school.

Because studying is often a lonely process, the companionship of people who meet at regular times to get their work done will be valued by all. The study area should be set up to allow for quiet concentration, with an additional space where people can work together without disturbing others.

Often, when you are stuck on a problem, you'll be able to solve it better if you can find someone to listen while you think it through. Even if the other person doesn't understand the problem, the mental work you do while explaining it, will cause you to notice connections you might have otherwise missed.

In study groups, people can share their successes. Good study habits are learned. You'll be able to discover what works for your friends, while sharing with them what works for you. You'll be building a support system to teach each other to be good students.

EVERY STUDY GROUP SHOULD HAVE A LEADER

It's important that every support group have an agreement not to let its members fall into bad habits. If the study group is an excuse for engaging in activities or talking about things that have nothing to do with study, it will be worse than useless.

Therefore, it's wise to have someone in charge who has good habits and refuses to let things deteriorate. The leader should enforce the rules of good study and ask others to leave if they slip into bad habits. Having one person to protect the group is essential.

You might want to rotate the role of leader every few weeks so each member has a turn. Responsibilities — like good study habits — must be learned, so it's good to give each member a chance to learn them. For example, it may be hard to ask your friend who is disturbing others in the study area to leave, but that's what all the members will expect the leader to do.

OTHER ROLES GROUP MEMBERS CAN TAKE

One way to develop leadership in study groups is to give every member a leadership role. In a study group of several people, give out or share the following roles: convener, moderator, sergeant-at-arms, note-taker, reporter, and encourager.

The convener's job is to see that the group meets regularly. If meetings have to be rescheduled, the convener contacts everyone and arranges a time. If there has not been a meeting for a while, the convener reminds people to come at the appropriate time. At the beginning of the meeting, the convener reports to the group if anyone is going to be late or missing.

The moderator's job is to lead the group through any discussion that needs to take place. This can include setting up rules for the group to follow, discussions of the material the group is studying, or discussions in preparation for a test. It might also include discussions of skills needed to study more effectively, such as learning to read better, take better notes, or write better papers.

The job of the sergeant-at-arms is to see that all the rules agreed to by the group are consistently observed by all members. This can include rules of discussion when there is discussion, and rules of behavior at other times.

The note-taker's job is to keep track of everything agreed to by the group and to take notes on discussion. These notes must be kept clearly enough so anyone can read and understand them.

The reporter's job is to read through the notes and report to the group about conclusions they have reached, perhaps reviewing the important points of earlier discussions. If the study group ever has to make a report to the whole class, or to any other group, the reporter would make that report, or at least organize its presentation.

The encourager's job is to cheer everyone on in their quest for excellence in the subjects of study, and to provide support and positive feedback for group and individual effort. This may be a role in which only one group member or everyone participates. It requires the same effort as cheerleading a football game; it rallies the players to succeed in the goal of winning the game — or, in this case, improving grades and study skills.

STEPS FOR SETTING UP A GROUP

Since forming a support group may be one of the most important things you can do to help yourself, let's take a little time here to think through what's involved in getting the group going.

FIRST: WHAT ARE YOUR GOALS

The first step is to be clear about what you want a support group to do for you. This can be anything you decide you want it to be, but for the purposes of this discussion, let's say you decide to form a group to help get your homework done.

So write down on paper exactly what you want the group to accomplish for you. Be as specific as you can. (There might be several different things you want from the group. If so, list all of them.)

CHOOSING MEMBERS OF THE GROUP

Once you're clear about what you want the group to do, think about the people you know who might share your interest in such a group. These should be people you like and would enjoy working with, but they don't necessarily have to be your present social group or your best friends.

When you've thought about this for a while, write down the names of about five people who might share with you an interest in forming a support group for study purposes.

Make sure you share the same goals

Wait a few days before you contact any of them. Meanwhile, think it over until you're sure you've got the list you really want. Are these people who really do want to accomplish what you want to accomplish? You might want to observe them and notice whether they seem to have in mind the goals you're considering.

After you've decided on your list and thought about it for a few days, (perhaps changing some of the names as you reconsider), start asking the people whether they'd like to join you in forming a support group. Tell them what you have in mind, and share your ideas with them about what the group should accomplish. For example, if the purpose of the group is to help get your homework done, look for people who, like you, might need a little help getting their work done on time.

SETTING THE TIME AND PLACE

After you've found several people who would like to join you in forming the group, select three times when you could get together with them, and ask each person which of those times would not be good for him or her. You will probably find at least one time when everyone can come to a short meeting.

Arrange for a place for this meeting and inform everyone where it is to be. You might want to bring the form on the next page to your first meeting and fill it out as a group.

POINTS TO COVER AT THE STUDY GROUP'S FIRST MEETING

Goals of Study Group _____

_____

_____

_____

_____

Possible Members _____

_____

_____

_____

Time to meet _____

Place to meet _____

Roles of Members (One person may need to take more than one role)

Leader _____

Convenor _____

Moderator _____

Sergeant-at-arms _____

Notes-Taker _____

Reporter _____

Encourager _____

Agenda _____

_____

_____

_____

_____

_____

_____

_____

Use lots of techniques in your study group:
- **Mind Maps**
- **Think-and-Listens**
- **Memorable stories**
- **Memory pegs**
- **Pictures, diagrams, posters**
- **Songs and raps**

When everyone comes, ask for ideas about how to make the support group work most effectively. Write down all the ideas and discuss them. Keep only those everyone agrees on.

Next, show the people who have attended the meeting the description of various roles given in the previous section. Discuss with them what role each person should have, and how it will be performed.

Next decide on a regular meeting time and place and agree on your first meeting.

Your final job for this meeting is to agree on an agenda, a list of things to be done at each meeting.

A SAMPLE AGENDA FOR A STUDY GROUP

For example, if the purpose of the group is to help each other get homework done, you might have the following agenda:

1. Each person lists all the homework assignments for the time period (day, week or term) involved.

2. Each person prioritizes the homework. That is, you decide what you're going to do first, what next, and so on, until you've accounted for all the assignments.

3. The group decides whether there is to be any type of help or discussion during the period of the meeting, or whether everyone is to study silently. It may be, for example, that two members would decide to work together on their math. Or perhaps the entire group would like to review for a test by asking each other questions. Possibly it would be appropriate to use some of the time listening to one member who is having problems with a course and wants help from the others in thinking about what to do.

4. The group decides whether there will be any breaks during the meeting, so people can walk around, go to the bathroom, get something to eat, or discuss what they are doing.

5. At the end of the session the members take time to share what they have accomplished during their time together and how they felt about each of the things they accomplished.

6. The members should also take time to evaluate the meeting to see whether there is some way they would like to improve the next meeting. If they do this well, the meetings are more likely to continue for as long as they can be helpful.

WHEN YOU'VE FALLEN BEHIND

If you work in a support group like this, you're much more likely to keep up with what you have to accomplish. But sometimes it may happen that you fall behind anyway, so let's go back to the idea of recovering from mistakes.

If you've fallen behind or failed at something, you should take steps to catch up. You don't always know what these are, but you can find out. It should help you at this point to review the problem solving skills we've explored in previous chapters, and see how you can apply them to the problem of catching up. For example, by making a list of good questions about the task or subject you've failed in, you can discover what you need to know to improve the situation.

The problem could be that the task or failure seems overwhelming. There is just too much you don't understand. It seems impossible ever to catch up.

The best way to overcome that difficulty is to make a schedule for catching up. Decide what the task involves, how much time it will take, and what you need to do to accomplish it. Then set realistic goals on a day-by-day basis. Make sure these are goals you can reach with a reasonable expenditure of time and effort. Otherwise, you'll probably get discouraged and give up.

Then write out an hour-by-hour schedule, showing what you intend to do when. If you get off schedule, revise your original schedule, and keep doing so until you have one that works.

This means you have to break down the task into its component parts. By doing so, you'll see much more clearly what's needed, and the problem will no longer seem so overwhelming. You'll also be able to decide on a sequence for your actions.

If you have trouble breaking the task into component parts, find someone who can help you — a fellow student or a teacher (perhaps not even your regular teacher). The point is to get feedback that will help you decide how to do whatever is needed.

In doing all these things, you will be applying the principles taught in this book to help you become the outstanding student you are so brilliantly capable of being.

Try This 👉 Get together with a friend who is feeling defeated by a problem. Have a talk and help him or her to find a solution.

12

Making Your Peace With The Clock

In this chapter you'll get a chance to think about how you relate to time. You'll learn a lot of strategies for organizing time, and you'll think about getting over your negative feelings about time (if you have any of those). But there's more to dealing with time than strategies — namely, getting the feeling of relaxing with the flow of time — so we'll try to help you with that too.

Probably nothing gets people in more trouble than the clock. Time is something all of us almost always wish we had more of (except when we're in a boring situation and wish we had less). We often plan to do too many things in too short a time, with the result that nothing gets done as well as we'd like.

CAN TIME REALLY BE MANAGED?

There are two apparently opposite things you can do about time. One is carefully plan your use of it, and the other is not to plan at all, but to "go with the flow." You should do both.

The way to accomplish this seemingly contradictory task is to plan your time well, but to allow your plan to be changed as opportunities appear which you couldn't have foreseen.

PROCRASTINATION AND FEAR

First we must recognize that many people put off an assignment because they simply can't bring themselves to do some part of it. There are any number of things that can arouse this kind of feeling. Unfortunately, some of those things may seem essential to the people who assigned the task or project.

> There's Always A Way To Make A Task Enjoyable

The fear or dislike of doing even one small part of an assignment may keep you from starting at all. A task that may look like a tiny chore to somebody else can look like a huge, insurmountable obstacle to you. It may be a fear of asking for help or a favor. Maybe it's fear of failure or rejection or simply a dislike for some person you need to consult.

Too often people let their feelings stop them from getting things done.

This makes them believe they don't have enough time, when in reality they do, but they're not using it well because of feelings or other distractions. They are afraid to do some essential little thing, and as a result, cannot complete a larger task. Many of us have this trouble in relation to doing an assignment, getting some information we need, or writing a paper that is overdue.

LEARNING TO CONTROL YOUR ANXIETY

If this problem arises, there are manageable steps you can follow in thinking through the sources of anxiety and then overcoming the fear:

1) Analyze exactly what it is you find threatening about what you are not getting done.

2) Figure out the worst thing that could happen in the situation you find so threatening. Will you be axe-murdered? Will you be humiliated? Will you flunk out of school? Will you find out that your One and Only doesn't love you after all?

3) How likely is it that the worst possible thing will be the thing that actually happens? What is the basis for believing that this will occur? Is this belief based on a judgment of other people that may be incorrect?

4) If there is some possibility of the worst happening, is there a way to prevent it? Is there a way to arrange things so that instead of having the worst happen you can have things work out the way you want them to?

5) Assuming that the worst happens, what alternatives are possible?

6) And if it really does happen, will it be possible to live through it?

What's the worst thing that could happen?

GETTING EMOTIONAL BLOCKS OUT OF THE WAY

Have you ever noticed that you always seem to have enough time to eat a bit of your favorite snack, to watch your favorite TV show, talk to your best friend, or lie around in bed a little longer. The things you probably don't have time for include doing the chores around the house, getting your homework done, and writing thank you notes. We usually get something done if we love doing it.

The important thing to recognize is that to a great extent you do control your time. If there's something keeping you from doing what you know you should do, it isn't time — it's you.

So its important to understand the reasons why you don't get certain things done. What emotional blocks are preventing you from handling time well? If you can analyze your problem for yourself, you may be well on your way toward solving it.

YOU MIGHT WANT TO GET A SECOND OPINION

Sometimes, though, it's easier to analyze someone else's problem than your own. So if you can't figure out how to get something important done, it might be a good idea to find someone else who has a similar problem and talk it over after both of you have agreed not to betray any confidences. You'll probably find that two or more heads are better than one in such matters.

Once you have confronted your problems with getting the important things done, and decided what to do in order to solve them, there are a number of practical and useful ways to think about time.

PRACTICAL APPROACHES TO DEALING WITH TIME

Let's consider some of the most important ones:

1) ***Schedules, lists, and priorities.*** In other words, write it down and commit yourself to it. Some people like to keep detailed calendars and plan their days hour by hour. Others like to make brief notes of what they are planning. The important thing is to think about what you definitely want to get done, and when you are going to do it.

2) ***Stop wasting short amounts of time.*** It's possible to do something of value while waiting for the bus, filling time between classes, or standing in line. What you choose to do with this time is up to you. You might want to use it to let your mind wander and be free of the pressure of structured activities. That's okay. But in that case, make a definite decision you're going to spend your time that way — don't just stand around aimlessly, wasting it.

If you really wanted to, you could use a five-minute block of time to go over your notes once more, review something you need to memorize, think about a paper you've been assigned to write — or lots of other things that are often better done in a short time between other tasks than in a longer time, when they may just get tangled up in confusion.

3) ***Estimate your time realistically.*** If you usually guess wrong about how long it's going to take you to do something, then you should recognize this fact and do something about it. Perhaps everything always seems to take three times as long as you thought it would. In that case, when you make your plans, decide how much time you think you'll need and triple it. If you handle this problem well, you'll nearly always have enough time for what you've planned to do, except when unexpected events interfere with your plans.

4) ***Don't try to do too many things at once.*** This usually happens because you can't decide what's most important, maybe because you want to do for others more than you're willing to do for yourself. Space out some of your activities more, say no to others, and break down large projects into smaller, more manageable pieces.

5) ***Plan ahead.*** Sometimes important papers and tests are scheduled in several different classes at the same time, which might mean you have to juggle your time a little more than usual. You can avoid this problem by planning ahead. Some assignments can be done long before they are due, and thus gotten out of the way. You may be able to spend less time on some projects than you think you have to. The pressure of too much to do will help you learn to skim, take more efficient notes, make intelligent guesses about things you aren't sure about, and read faster.

6) **Don't fight yourself.** Sometimes when you sit down to work you may feel too tired to concentrate well. You should know when your high- and low-energy periods occur and schedule things accordingly. Don't attempt a task at a time when you're going to fall asleep trying to get it done.

7) **Step back.** Some things can take a lot more time than they should. If you find you're spending seven hours doing one math problem, it's probably time to step back and get a little perspective. Vary your activities more, get help where it's needed, find out what background information you're lacking, and take breaks — sometimes, if necessary, for sleeping.

8) **Finish what you start.** Sometimes you can get into the rut of never finishing projects that you start. Make it a priority to finish a project once you embark on it, provided it's of value, even if you have many projects going at once. Starting projects and not finishing them wastes more time than most other things. Plan your important projects so you can finish them.

9) **Plan your place.** Seek out the conditions that make you feel most alert and able to focus on your work. If you're the kind of person who falls asleep while studying in bed, or on a couch, sit up at a desk or table. you'll get more done if you maintain upright posture. On the other hand, if you are the kind of person who can't concentrate when you sit in hard, unyielding furniture; find a more comfortable place. Locate your study area in a place where you enjoy studying and can concentrate well. There should be no more noise and other distractions than you're comfortable with. If you can't study without some music or background noise, turn on a radio or wear headphones. If you prefer quiet, then don't sit in the hallway at school during recess and expect to get anything done. If the people at home distract you, go to the library.

10) **Get organized.** Living in a messy environment can cause you to waste a lot of time looking for things. A little time spent each day getting organized, putting things away, maintaining your files and doing routine daily chores will save a lot of time in the long run. Form the habit of preparing your study area before beginning work. Get everything you'll need together so you don't have to interrupt yourself. Many of us have messy work areas in order to avoid completing things. Watch out that you don't use this as an excuse.

11) **Avoid interruptions.** You can waste a whole evening if you're interrupted all the time. Don't attempt to study where there are people or telephones that constantly demand your attention. One emergency interruption per week is okay, not six every night. You have a right to your quiet times — don't let others intrude on them.

BUILD YOUR OWN PROGRAM OF TIME CONSERVATION FROM THESE SUGGESTIONS

If you start implementing some of these ideas now, you'll find you have a lot more time to use as you wish. The clock doesn't have to be your enemy. When you've made peace with what you have to do,.you'll find it's possible to keep a very busy schedule and still feel as if you have enough time to do all the things you want to do.

Here are three ways I'll improve my use of time:

_____

_____

_____

GOING WITH THE FLOW

And that brings us to the second part of this two-part approach to time management. Once you're used to planning your schedule and can do that well, you'll be in a better position to let things unfold in their own way. You'll discover the joy of always being in the present time, responding to what is actually happening instead of worrying about what has happened or might happen.

If you know that you can control time, you'll be ready to begin letting go of it and responding to the shifting needs of the moment. Controlling time should become so easy that you no longer feel you're controlling it at all, but are just taking things as they come. Once you've had a taste of this, you'll find it gets easier to sense what really needs to be done, and you'll be able to get to it when appropriate.

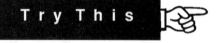

Try This

Find an area of your life where you're not managing time well; one where you either spend more time or less time than you should. Explore ways to get that part of your life in control.

13

The Power Of Story-Telling And The Value Of Dreaming

Shakespeare said, "We are such stuff as dreams are made on," and in this chapter we'll look at what an important role dreams can play in your life, and how the way you daydream and tell stories to yourself can affect your success.

There are many ways to visualize and imagine things, but unfortunately we don't usually learn much about these in school. So here's a chance to get to know your eyes, how they work, and how they can work together with your mind's eye to make you a more brilliant student. Then you'll see that what you believe about yourself and what you see for yourself in the future is quite important. You'll see how true it is that you can do whatever you think you can.

THE UNIVERSE DOESN'T OWE YOU A LIVING

There is an old expression that "life is what you make it." It might be better to say that "life is what you think it." Because how you think about it directly influences what you make it. That's hard for some people to understand, for there are many who believe that what happens in your life is the fault of someone else — perhaps the universe itself. This poem by Stephen Crane shows how foolish that idea is:

A Man Said to the Universe
by Stephen Crane

A man said to the universe:
"Sir, I exist!"
"However," replied the universe,
"The fact has not created in me
"A sense of obligation."

No, if we are to be successful in life we must achieve success on our own, we cannot ask the universe to do it for us. On the other hand, if we use our minds properly, they can help us be successful.

Perhaps you remember the story of **The Little Engine That Could**, in which the little engine looked ahead to climbing the mountain and said, "I think I can, I think I can, I think I can." After much effort, but also a belief in herself and her vision, the little engine reached the top, and was able to coast down the other side, exclaiming, "I thought I could, I thought I could, I thought I could."

GET BUSY DAYDREAMING AND STORYTELLING!

One of the most important secrets of success is creative and effective daydreaming. Unfortunately, many of us have learned that daydreaming is not a good idea. Perhaps we've been led to believe it's lazy or inattentive. Yet creative daydreaming is one of the most important tools we can use to make a better future for ourselves.

Just for an instant, raise your eyes from the page of this book and look around you. Is there anything you can see (other than nature's beauty) that did not exist in the mind and imagination of some inventor before it took shape as an object in reality?

Behind every creative act there is a vision, or daydream, which had to be imagined before it could become reality. The world's greatest leaders have been among its greatest dreamers. It is only those who lead routine lives, never imagining anything wonderful or experiencing anything new, who do not daydream.

Often it is in the stories we "write" for ourselves that we create the dreams that can make our future. If you imagine you will never make much of your life, that is probably what will happen.

But if you imagine yourself reaching a goal that is important to you, and use your daydreams to work out how that goal can be reached, then you've greatly increased the likelihood that eventually you'll reach it. Dreams alone will not work, of course, because you must also do something to transform them into reality. But the dreams point the way and get the process started.

People have long suspected that how you think, your state of awareness, your consciousness, and your awareness of your possibilities, can make all the difference in creating **your** reality and increasing your success — whatever you do. And in recent times modern medicine and science have verified and begun to explore how our minds influence our overall health. No one knows for sure how or why it works, but the fact that it does has now been demonstrated scientifically.

LEARNING TO SEE IN YOUR MIND'S EYE

Suppose you want to build a table. Of course you can't build a table unless you first have an idea of what it's going to look like. To get that idea, you can either follow a set of directions or look at a picture.

Or you can make your own picture in your mind's eye and follow that. Did you know that when you open your eyes and look at something, most of the job of seeing it happens in your brain?

Have you ever been told to stop daydreaming?

**Start With A Dream --
Make It A Reality**

SEEING WITH YOUR EYES CLOSED

In order for your brain to receive messages from your eyes, they must first register the impact of light rays on the retina at the back of your eye. These responses of the retina are turned into a series of impulses that pass through the optic nerve. The brain then, by some mysterious means, translates the impulses into the impression you see as a picture. The picture-making part of the brain is thus not in the eyes and not in the optic nerve, but is something altogether different.

In other words, you don't have to have your eyes open in order to see pictures. Your brain can make pictures equally well with or without getting information from your eyes. All it takes is practice for your brain to become just as good at inventing pictures as it is at "seeing" them.

If you can remember dreams, you have seen pictures with your eyes closed. You can also see pictures just by imagining them. For example, if I ask you to imagine . . . *you are walking down the road, the sun is bright, it's shining on your face, and brilliantly lighting a meadow of wildflowers* . . . you can probably see that field in your mind's eye, feel the warmth of the sun on your cheek.

Visualizing Taps Your Brain's Power To Find Creative Solutions

The main reason the pictures you see with your eyes closed are not as vivid as those you see with your eyes open is that you practice visualizing with your eyes open many hours each day, but the practice you have visualizing with your eyes closed may be no more than a few minutes each night. If you were to practice visualizing with your eyes closed, you could probably learn to do it pretty well.

SEEING YOUR FUTURE

And what is the point of trying to "see" with our eyes closed? The point is that what we see in this way can have a powerful influence over our behavior, and consequently over our lives.

By using this kind of seeing, we can make what we believe or hope is possible become real. So, our vision, purpose and direction as imagined in the stories we write in our minds can have great impact on our achievement.

The achievement may be a simple, practical thing like planning your day or making an improvement in your schoolwork; but it can also help you with long term goals, such as imagining what you want to do with your life, planning your college program, or improving your social relationships. Such things are essential if you want to do anything creative.

So daydream frequently. Find a place where you won't be disturbed. Put on some music (Baroque, Classical or Romantic music will provide the best sound environment), and then relax. Let go of any tension in your muscles and allow a steady stream of positive images to enter your mind. These images may provide the key to a problem you are having now.

Don't force this. It's not a chore -- it only works when you're enjoying it.

It may not be an immediate solution, but many creative and highly disciplined thinkers have found that a solution will sometimes occur unexpectedly in this way if they allow their minds to freely play with the problem.

Have you ever tried an exercise like this? Before you decide how you feel about it, give it a try.

GET OUT THE PENCIL TOO

You may want to keep records of your daydreams by writing them down in an expandable story form. Then you can build up the story whenever you practice your visualizations. Or you may wish to explore it more actively and practically, looking for things you can do to make your story come true. There's a simple method called Expand-a-Story that can help you write the story of your success.

EXPAND-A-STORY

1. Write down the elements of your story. Where are you when the story begins? What goals do you reach? What events help you reach the goal? What accomplishments or skills do you acquire along the way? What problems do you confront? What plot twists and suprises do you work out to solve the problems?

2. Arrange the story elements in the best order. Leave plenty of room between parts of the story. Then you can add to it as ideas and new plans occur to you.

3. Look for gaps in the plot, places where the story is weak or not very believable. Add the missing pieces —events or accomplishments that make it seem more real and believable. (These might not occur to you immediately but if you keep on daydreaming and creatively thinking about your story, the solutions will eventually come to you.)

4. Keep refining and enriching your story. As important new goals, new ideas, and new events happen in your life, add them to the story, see where they fit in.

YOUR PERSONAL FRONT ROW SEAT

Some people get upset because they close their eyes and try to imagine what they are thinking about, only to feel they can't actually "see" anything. If this happens to you, there's a simple technique you can use to overcome this feeling.

Pretend you're sitting in a theater watching a play, only the curtain is down. The play is taking place behind the curtain. You imagine it without being able to see it.

If you imagine the scene this way, you will get over feeling you have to "see" it in the same way you see with your eyes open. You'll feel in your imagination what it would be like without necessarily seeing actual pictures, and that's good enough.

GREAT SEERS

Histories are written about many great leaders, athletes, inventors and public servants, who first imagined and saw themselves carrying out the seemingly difficult tasks they achieved.

Before he set foot on the Olympic track in Germany in 1936, Jesse Owens imagined himself standing with Olympic medals glistening around his neck and with the American Flag waving high in celebration of his victory.

As recently as 1960, few people thought it possible that a human could ever set foot on the moon. It took a visionary like President John F. Kennedy to inspire a nation to "think " it possible, making it a reality in 1968.

BELIEFS CAN HOLD YOU BACK

Just the opposite occurs also. Some years ago, most of the runners and sports experts in the world believed it was physically impossible to run a mile in under four minutes. After this goal was finally achieved, many were able to run the mile in less than four minutes. What had happened to the four minute barrier? Where had the barrier been in the first place?

HOW SOCIAL NORMS CAUSE TROUBLE

One of the major blocks to achievement is the belief system shared by most members of a group, society or culture. If all the people around you believe something is impossible, you are unlikely to try it or believe that it can be done. If you do try, even you may start thinking you're crazy.

Social norms can have the good effect of protecting the group from harmful or disgusting behavior. But when they prevent or inhibit people from attempting good things, as they often do, these norms can actually imprison the group and prevent everyone from having a better life.

HOW ABOUT A NEW SET OF NORMS?

Suppose you tried to imagine a classroom, a school, a whole society that would be the way you thought it should be. And suppose you made a list of what you liked about that improved society, and the list included some of these things:

> Everyone in the class doing A work and receiving an A.
>
> Everyone in the class being treated with equal respect.
>
> Boys and girls always treating each other in ways that are fully human.
>
> People who don't look like movie stars being regarded as attractive.
>
> Everyone respecting the good of the whole human race instead of only what is best for them as individuals.
>
> Everyone knowing and experiencing that their quality of life does not depend on what ethnic group they belong to.

Are these the social norms in your present group and society? If not, why not? Do they look like an impossible dream? Why?

What other attitudes could improve life around you?

SOCIAL NORMS AND RACIAL PREJUDICE

Probably the worst effect of social norms is to create stereotypes, and these can be dangerous and destructive to whole groups of people. The acceptance of the notion that one group or race of people is less good, less human, than another opens the door to terrible injustice and tragedy. The belief that African-Americans, Spanish-speaking Americans, Native Americans, Asian-Americans — or any group — is inferior to any other has had tragic effects in our society, and will continue to have terrible consequences until it is changed.

Unfortunately, this belief in the inferiority of certain groups, is held not only by their oppressors, but often by some members of the groups themselves. In other words, if the social norm is strong enough, the prejudice can be internalized, can be turned into prejudice against oneself.

ARE YOU PREJUDICED AGAINST YOURSELF?

In fact, nearly everyone is prejudiced against him or herself in at least a few ways. Try to make a list right now of the ways in which you are prejudiced against yourself.

Some of your prejudice might be obvious. Here are some possibilities to check out:

❑　I am not attractive enough.

❑　I am too fat or too thin.

❑　My nose is the wrong shape.

❑　I am not "cool".

❑　My ideas are not worth much.

❑　Most people don't like me very much.

I wish I could do something about the color of my: (check one or more)

❑　skin,　　❑　hair,　　❑　eyes.

But there are other, more subtle types of self-prejudice, having to do with what we think we are capable of. The following are worth checking out:

❑　I can't draw.

❑　I can't sing.

❑　I can't speak in front of an audience.

❑　I can't make good conversation.

❑　I can't do math.

❑　I can't write a decent paragraph.

❑　I can't remember things.

❑　I can't do homework.

❑　I can't hit a baseball.

❑　I can't get along with others.

❑　I can't get a better job.

THE ART AND SCIENCE OF I-CAN'T-OLOGY

These are examples of "Icantology," the study of not being able to do things. This business of not being able to do things is almost a virus among students, a disease that spreads among them everywhere.

Each of us has used "I can't" statements to justify how we think about all sorts of things we believe are impossible. When we use "I can't," we create a story, an expectation of negativity and self-doubt. And, sadly, we tend to live up — or down — to our own expectations of ourselves. Whatever we think we can't do we will probably fail to do, even though it might actually be easy if only we went about it the right way.

Unfortunately, school and other learning experiences too often accomplish the exact opposite of what they are supposed to do. Instead of learning how to do things, we are left with the impression that we can't ever hope to learn them.

If school worked really well for you, you would learn everything anyone is trying to teach. When it doesn't work well, you learn little, or perhaps almost nothing. In general, school will work better for you if you expect it to, because you believe deep in your heart that you **can** learn. To reinforce this belief, **see** yourself being able to do the things you want to be able to do.

HOW TO WIN THE OLYMPICS

Or, take a leaf out of the book of Olympic athletes. When they prepare for their events, they go through a mental rehearsal, visualizing each step of the competition. They feel in their bodies, as if it were really happening, the moment-by-moment activity that is for them the pursuit of excellence.

> It's a proven fact: Mental rehearsal actually improves physical performance.

Champion golfer Jack Nicklaus visually writes a story before each shot. He sees himself in the shot, hears the ball, sees the rise and watches it land on the green. After that experience, he actually steps up and hits the ball.

The world famous tennis star and United States Davis Cup Coach, Arthur Ashe, visualized himself beating each of the best players, stroke by stroke, until he finally became the first American of African ancestry to win the championship at Wimbledon.

These are not just notable testimonials of famous people. Rather they are examples of what many people think is the essence of unlocking the genius in us all.

GUIDE YOUR OWN IMAGERY

Daydream — create your own life story. Practice as you're dropping off to sleep at night. See in your mind pleasant images that help you to relax and feel a natural enjoyment of life. After you've done this for a while, you'll be better able to do it whenever you want to relax your mind in order to study or do anything else that requires deep concentration.

As Helen Keller said, "Be adventuresome." Your education is too important to leave to anyone but yourself. You have the tools to create your many fruitful new possibilities. Use the tools you've learned about in this book for the rest of your life. They'll help you be more and more successful every day in reaching your goals.

Success isn't something that depends entirely on you. Luck plays a part too. But if you're thinking well about being successful, luck will go with you in the long run.

And as you continue to apply what you've learned here, you'll think of many other things you can do to increase your chances of success.

There's an old motto you've probably seen many times in safety programs. It goes: "The life you save may be your own." We'd like to conclude by changing it just a little. Try it this way: "The life you create will be your own."

About the Authors

Peter Kline is a pioneer in applying the best and most advanced understanding of the dynamics of learning to classroom, workplace, and home. He is one of the most creative, experienced and respected leaders in the field of Integrative Learning, a new educational philosophy that when applied, produces dramatic improvements in student performance.

As an author and consultant, much in demand throughout the country, he has created innovative courses and trained teachers in the use of non-traditional methods that accelerate learning and bring joy and excitement to the classroom. His work has been described by one journalist as "the miracle cure for the nation's schools."

Peter Kline is the author of many publications on education and theater. His widely praised 1989 book, THE EVERYDAY GENIUS, introduces the principles of Integrative Learning to a popular audience, and has been made a main selection of the NEA Professional Book Club. He resides with his family in South Bend, Indiana.

✦ ✦ ✦

Dr. Laurence Martel currently the president of the National Academy of Integrative Learning, is a leader in the movement to revitalize education in America. He envisions an America of self-directed lifelong learners. As such, Dr. Martel and the National Academy seek to redefine schools as communities that draw out the genius in all students through the development of individual learning power.

Formerly on the faculty of Syracuse University where he was a director of the Center for Learning and Retention, Dr. Martel has created and implemented numerous programs to teach students how to significantly increase their school performance. His work is internationally recognized and has been funded by various governmental and private foundations. He has served as a consultant to several governments, State Education Departments and major corporations.

Dr. Martel is the author of many academic publications and has been a contributor to many journals of higher education. He resides with his family in Hilton Head Island, South Carolina.

About the Publisher

Great Ocean Publishers, Inc., is a publishing company dedicated to providing innovative educational materials of proven value in all media. We welcome comments and suggestions from readers and users of our publications and products.

GREAT OCEAN PUBLISHERS, INC.
1823 North Lincoln Street
Arlington, VA 22207
(Phone: 703-525-0909)